D1564263

SMITHSON'S ISLAND
THE NECESSITY OF SOLITUDE

BY
JUDITH ANN SMITHSON

LONE OAK PRESS, LTD.

SMITHSON'S ISLAND
THE NECESSITY OF SOLITUDE

BY
JUDITH ANN SMITHSON

PUBLISHED
BY
LONE OAK PRESS, LTD.
304 11TH AVENUE SOUTHEAST
ROCHESTER, MINNESOTA 55904–7221

First Edition
Second Printing March 1997
ISBN NUMBER 1–883477–08–5
LIBRARY OF CONGRESS CARD CATALOG NUMBER 95–081508

To Tony

"When from our better selves we have too long
Been parted by the hurrying world, and droop,
Sick of its business, of its pleasures tired,
How gracious, how benign, is Solitude."

William Wordsworth, "The Prelude"

FOREWORD

This journal of simplicity and solitude speaks to all of us about the complexity of our lives. As Judy Smithson brings us on an external journey through the seasons of the year, she also guides us through an interior journey that beckons us to contemplate our priorities. Her insights are personal, but universal for those who choose to live deliberately, as Thoreau suggests.

The reading of Judy's journal will speak clearly to those who are in an especially hurried time in their lives. It offers the motivation to reflect, to realize that the world allows little space for solitude, and to choose a way to achieve solitude on a personal level.

One becomes convinced, as Judy says so well in her book, that "solitude's essence resides within us, wherever we might be." With practice, perhaps we can all locate a quiet place within ourselves no matter how hurried the pace of life might be. This is indeed a credit to Judy and to her willingness to share her inner journey.

Dr. Robert R. Waller, M.D.

TABLE OF CONTENTS

PREFACE

This journal records four trips into solitude in 1992. I planned the visits and this journal to follow the seasons and spent a week each season at a northern Minnesota island.

My inspiration for these journeys came from some writers who explored the individual's relationship to the natural world. I discovered that most of them wrote in solitude in a particular landscape. Henry Thoreau's was Walden Pond, near Concord, Massachusetts; Annie Dillard's, Tinker Creek, in Virginia's Blue Ridge. Anne Truitt's, Yaddo, in Sara Toga Springs, New York. What emerged out of their experiences was a wealth of discovery: self knowledge, social awareness, an affinity with the natural world, and creativity.

Anne Truitt's journey in *DAYBOOK, The Journal of An Artist* particularly engaged me. She not only examined her art and its value, but also confronted her life, her childhood, her career decisions, her children's journeying into adulthood, her failed marriage. Most profound was her unceasingly honest self examination which arose out of solitude at Yaddo or in her bed in the early morning. After considering the fruits Truitt gleaned from solitude, I was persuaded to investigate its character and discover mine.

Time for such an undertaking was limited by family and work responsibilities. I settled on four separate weeks dispersed through the seasons. Aware that the changing seasons affect us all, I was curious how I would respond to their differences.

My family is fortunate to share ownership of an island on Whitefish Lake in Northern Minnesota. It provided both the landscape and the solitude I was seeking. My shelter was a log cabin. Though it lacked winter plumbing and a furnace, it did have electricity and a woodstove for winter.

In the course of my visits this journal reached its present form. The pages record the manner in which I spent my days, my discoveries and my reflections. As a woman at 49, my viewpoints reflect my stage in life. Like Truitt, I discovered solitude fosters a turning to one's interior landscape. Solitude also possesses its own validity which insists on honest confrontation. I confronted not only who I am, but also my marriage, my children, my art, my spirituality, and my future. Because I recorded each day as I lived it, this book is essentially a diary, not a literary endeavor. It does not reflect a particular theme beyond that of a woman's experience in solitude. I suspect many women in their middle years will recognize and claim some of my observations as their own.

In looking back at my journeys, as brief as they were, I realize what a profound adventure I lived. I explored both the natural world and the character of solitude   imagining I would find a kind of paradise revealed in their synthesis. Immersing oneself in nature is a riveting experience. I discovered a re awakening of my senses and became Thoreau's "self appointed inspector of snow storms and rain storms." Awakening to birdsong ushering in the light, noticing the sublime blue of the autumn sky, or inhaling the pungent fragrance of damp woods in the evening set my spirits soaring. Such simple pleasures cost nothing. The gentle whisper of rain is free. Significant moments await us in nearby woods, a quiet park, a country road, even in our own neighborhoods and backyards.

The fruits of solitude are likewise available. We must simply take time alone. Solitude's gifts and insights do not require island landscapes or retreats, as lovely as they are. Most of us have early mornings or evenings we can call our own. Perhaps even a weekend. Each can be an island of solitude. I am convinced who we are alone may be as important as the relationships we consider important to our happiness before solitude renders a perspective where we can see ourselves whole.

It is my hope that this journal will lead readers to investigate the character of solitude and re discover the joys of the natural world. Both offer a venture into living more fully and more wisely. Each of us has a unique story to uncover and to explore. Our lives, like the seasons, know birth, growth, fruition, and death. Frequently I have neglected to ponder their significance. This is a record of the time when I didn't.

WINTER

Woodstove

I took to the road this morning heading north. Destination: Paradise. But not that of Kerouac's characters, Dean and Sal, who expected the ultimate in music or love or understanding around the next bend in the road. Their Paradise lay in a landscape of excitement, movement, and stimulants. They were ... "mad to live, mad to talk, mad to be saved, desirous of everything at the same time... "

At 49 I am no longer a fevered adolescent. My notion of Paradise resides in solitude. This is where I believe the pearl of self discovery and creativity is secreted. It waits in unlimited, unstructured time. In unencumbered space. In the natural world. Perhaps I shall discover a fragment of Eden in the synthesis of nature and solitude.

Geographically and personally I took to the road with an island destination. Islands more than any other landscape are refuges of solitude. They abound in mythology and literature as symbols of earthly paradise. In Celtic legends the Isles of the Blest were the eternal home of favored mortals when they died. Greek mythology called their island paradise the Elysian Fields. Annie Dillard was drawn to the Galapagos Islands of Darwinian fame, which claim creatures who "exist nowhere else on earth." She wrote of animals who were tame and unafraid, of finches who came when she called.

My island destination does not boast of the Galapagos wonders; nor is it steeped in the mythologies of Paradise. It lies in Whitefish Lake in northern Minnesota. It is a sanctuary of familiar wildlife and flora. But it promises solitude. Perhaps an undiscovered pearl. Perhaps a glimpse of Eden.

Fortified with my island imaginings I arrived at Whitefish Lake in the early afternoon after driving 300 miles. An hour from shore lay the island where I would spend seven days in solitude and return the succeeding seasons. I felt confident, even euphoric about my sojourn. I was one of Lillian Rubin's "women of a certain age," deconstructing the "empty nest" myth of the menopausal woman... the woman "incapable of either conceiving or desiring a 'room of her own.'" I was embarking on an adventure of risk and possibilities. My husband, Tony, and others, told me I was crazy to head up to an island alone in the hard cold of a Minnesota winter. I could break a leg and die in the cold. I would get lonely. Wouldn't I be afraid? What if I did not have the physical strength to auger into the frozen lake for water? What if the old woodstove could not warm the log cabin where I would be lodging? Stubbornly I dismissed their concerns. I was convinced none of these events would occur. And I was prepared.

All of them were mired in mistaken assertions of the middle aged woman's resolve. They did not know about my trappings. Before embarking on this journey I went to Fleet Farm. I purchased men's 40° Sorel boots and a man's wool jacket lined in sheepskin. I ignored the ladies' fashionable Carolina blue boots with their feminine collars of white fur. I ignored the pastel jackets designed for compliments. I set out to buy tough clothing, and the men's department sold it. I felt invincible. I needed to demythologize the feminine stereotype of vulnerability because I believed it was false. Men's "fashions" offered me this possibility, both physically and psychologically.

At the base of the hill leading to the lake I unloaded the car and piled two plastic sleds with my gear   a sleeping bag, a cooler, a duffle stuffed with books and clothing, an ice auger, a fire extinguisher, a food bag, a small heater to thaw the toilet plumbing, and two gallons of drinking water.

I laced and buckled my snowshoes. After a few steps they slipped off my shoes. I buckled them again. They slipped again. Frustrated, I laid them across the two sleds along with my duffle. Trudging up the hill through snow up to my knees, I tired quickly. The hill seemed interminable. I was panting. I felt dizzy. I couldn't quit. Not now, not after my vows of bravado. I had skipped lunch. That was the problem. Slowly I made headway. The hill's peak was only steps away. Soon gravity would be on my side, and indeed the sleds sailed down behind me to the lake's edge. I slumped on the duffle. Wearily I opened a loaf of bread and globbed Jif over a slice with my finger. I drank some juice. Soon I felt renewed and my breathing became regular again. I would not be rendered powerless by this landscape, but it had gained my respect. At least I was warm. My Fleet Farm purchases humbled the cold air.

Newly fallen snow covered the lake like a freshly primed canvas. It was so pristine I momentarily felt my presence was an intrusion. No human imprints were visible. No brushstrokes discernible. Just this endless smooth fabric of white. Beside me was the dock hidden in its winter sarcophagus. Only the tops of the snowcapped posts belied its presence. The posts reached out in precarious postures. Freezes and thaws had loosened the footings in their relentless seasonal rhythms.

I pulled the sleds onto the lake not knowing precisely where the land stopped and the lake began. The land's boundaries could only be perceived with certainty where dark trees, wet from last night's snow, swept across the landscape. Their strong simple forms were reminiscent of Franz Kline's powerful compositions in black and white.

The sleds were heavy and cumbersome as I started across the lake. Again I felt my heart accelerate as I pulled the load through the deep snow. Every step was a march and my thighs soon ached. I stopped to rest. Standing in the middle of the lake I surveyed my surroundings. Nothing was moving. Not a bird. Not a branch. The world slumbered around me. The steel gray sky yawned heavily with sleep; even the distant shore was a soft gesture of repose. The silence filled my ears with its immense quiet. I was looking solitude in the eye and confronting its mute language.

Not far ahead was the small island before ours. The spruce and firs once black gradually changed to deep green. Nearing the island's tip I spotted deer tracks, now rounded from the fresh snow. I was elated to know there were living creatures nearby, and wondered if they were watching me from hiding places. How incongruous I must seem to them pulling my orange and blue sleds across the lake. Rounding the island, I glimpsed the tobacco brown of our log cabin. New resolve and energy entered my body. I was beside the northwest tip of our island heading eastward. My steps now paralleled the island's shoreline. Visions of hot coffee and shelter quickened my pace. I knew I would make it. Hadn't I just walked on water?

I stepped onto the island and sank into a deep drift. This time the boundary of lake and land was dramatic though still invisible. The elements were still challenging me. So was the land whose incline to the cabin was too steep for my load which I could not budge. I carried up the duffle. With the load lightened I made my final ascent. I carried in logs for the woodstove, turned on the electricity, and lit the pilots on the stove. The cabin registered 20°F. Crumpled newspaper and birch logs were soon blazing. Wishing to preserve my water supply, I scooped up loose snow in a cooking pot. It produced an inch of water. After numerous additions of snow, I was sipping hot coffee. Then I stretched out in front of the woodstove where sleep overtook me. My coffee grew cold.

I was awakened by the thump of a log tumbling in the woodstove. After stoking the fire and adding more wood, I put on my Sorels and ventured outside into the deep white cold. I sank close to my knees. Snow had sculpted itself around the trees and whipped itself into waves around the cabin. A ribbon of black earth formed a moat under the cabin's eaves. My lodging was a fortress. I made my way to the wooded path leading westward to Birchwood cabin. This cabin is a five minute stroll in summer, invisible until you reach it. But this afternoon I sighted it easily. Winter had opened up the woods. I could turn 360° and never lose sight of the sky through the trees. The island felt like an island. In other seasons foliage blocks the view. I am surrounded by woods which could be anywhere. Even the path was transformed. Its former boundaries of lush ferns were now tight cinnamon bundles at my feet. It spilled into the young alders whose gangly stick forms seemed awkward in their nudity. An unfamiliar starkness defined my surroundings. Winter changed how I saw and what I saw. Nothing was tempered. Particularly not death. Death and dying riveted my attention with its complex crosshatching of leaning and broken trees. Some had decayed with age; others had submitted to storms greater than they. There was a fearful grotesqueness in their twisted timbers of violent death and a sadness where death came gently. But other trees heartened me as they rose gallantly among them, fingering the sky with their bare slender branches. They were suspended in time for the duration of winter. I walked on. Shortly I came upon miniature spruce and firs sprouting where trees had died. Celery colored lichens were growing on the decaying logs and shelf fungi marched bravely in caps of snow. Surely death was not to be mourned or feared here, for I saw the life it spawned. The ecological master plan was functioning. Perfectly. How could I have forgotten that the exquisite morels I seek in spring rise up near the roots of dead elms?

Chilled, I started back. One of the pleasures of cold is returning to warmth. The woodstove did not let me down. I changed into my old navy sweatsuit and hung my damp jeans on a clothesline behind the stove. After eating a frozen dinner whose container I could burn, the phone rang, jarring my solitude. It was Tony calling to see if I had made it safely. I assured him all was well. It was. At least it seemed to be.

On awakening I looked out the window. The view was heavily veiled by a fog whose soft edges reduced the landscape to a minimalist painting. The impression was a sublime aura of floating atmosphere. Lake and sky were blurred horizontal bands. No textures defined this abstract vista. It stretched across my entire field of vision, pulling me into an other worldly place. This was a landscape of lost definition. Mark Rothko's environmental canvases fleeted before my eyes and I wondered if he was once immersed in such a place as this.

A phone call drew me out of my reverie. It was our friend Byron Bromley on the mainland whom I had forgotten to call. Tony had asked that I check in with Byron each day. Byron was anxious about my welfare, for he knew I was to arrive yesterday and had not called to ask his help in crossing the lake. My explanation of handling this venture alone was uncharacteristic and unsettling. Byron is a powerful, gentle man whose relationship to our family is that of caretaker. Through the years we have always turned to him to assist with projects and solve problems. My solitary resolve did not fit our past narrative. "A woman should not be too independent," he admonished me. "It can be dangerous up here." I mused what dangers I should fear. A tree falling? A fire starting from the woodstove? I assured him I would be careful and would call promptly each morning at 8:00 am.

After a breakfast of coffee, juice, and bagels, I was eager to go walking before writing in this journal. I had solved my snowshoe dilemma. Loops I had never noticed are attached to my Sorels. How simple it was to slip the leather straps through them. Once buckled the snowshoes were secure. I set out through the woods with no destination in mind. After twice tripping over hidden logs I changed my tactics. Instead of walking aimlessly I took my cues from the deer whose paths meandered throughout the island. Were they not more knowledgeable than I about how to traverse these woods? I accepted this premise and successful snowshoeing ensued.

My only companion this morning was a profound silence. I heard nothing. No snapping of brittle twigs. No beating of air. Only the sounds of my breathing and crunching footsteps rippled the silence. Yet a rush of expectation filled me as I walked. Would a flock of starlings appear overhead? Would a snowhare dart in front of me? The deer tracks gave me heart. Their snow patterns confirmed I had neighbors on this island. But no deer ever appeared. Once Annie Dillard was also denied a deer sighting and noted, "Deer apparently ascend bodily into heaven." She too hoped nature would reveal its bounty but discovered instead its capacity to conceal.

This was a place of absence, or was it a place of resolution, reduced to its essence? There were no people. No odors. No sounds. No breeze. No sunshine. Not even my shadow joined me in my walking. I was suspended in time in a primordial landscape. I felt uniquely alone, yet strangely at ease in my aloneness. I discovered in this absence a capacity for solitude. I began re ordering my expectations. Being denied an encounter with any "life" did not lead to loneliness or despair. Quite the contrary occurred. I entered a kind of peaceful dormancy where I simply allowed these mute woods to fill me. My focus turned inward. I knew I could not speak the forest's language any more than I could speak the deer's. I was a vessel where absence became a quiet presence, where I became one with the woods.

I returned to the cabin anxious to write. Soon spent, I stretched out on the floor and napped until hunger roused me. While munching on cheese and crackers, I mulled over my afternoon plans of getting water. It was a necessity I could no longer put off. Toilets must be flushed. Reluctantly I grabbed the ice auger and snowshoed out a fair distance on the lake. If I augured in too shallow an area the lake might be frozen to the bottom. After clearing the snow cover, I exerted pressure on the auger as my husband had shown me and began turning. The sharp blades grabbed immediately, but my turning arm quickly tired, so I worked in spurts followed by rests. I could see I was making headway as the corkscrew shaft grew shorter. I pulled it out at about a foot and cleared away the finely shaved ice. Renewing my efforts I counted ten turns. Rest. Ten turns. Rest. I lost count. Suddenly I broke through! Black water spewed out of the hole. I jumped back. Pulling out the auger I discovered I had worked through almost three feet of ice. I began laughing. How satisfying it was to succeed! Others' doubts about my abilities were now avenged. Or had I avenged my own?

I returned to the cabin for two buckets and the hand pump. I slid the pump's longer tube into the hole and placed the shorter in one of the buckets. Then the work of turning the handle awaited me. Little did I know this would be as tiring as auguring. The pump was clumsy to hold and the water trickled in slowly. At last the bucket was full and I began filling the second one. It went even more slowly. By now my arm was trembling with fatigue. Finally, I started to the cabin with my treasure. Perhaps halfway, I sensed one bucket seemed lighter. I glanced down. It was two thirds empty. A leak I could not see was the culprit. Cursing my bad luck, I quickly poured the remaining water up to the brim of the good bucket. Wearily I trudged back. My euphoria had disappeared. But at least the toilet got flushed. One bucket was enough.

Now darkness blackens the windowpanes. I do not even know when the sun set, as the overcast skies have denied its power as a timekeeper. Even during the day I hardly noticed the light. It was somewhere else.

Feeling lethargic, I decided to snowshoe the lake to the southeast corner of the island. This is where the island is separated from the mainland by a mere four foot width of water, but it is not accessible to us for crossing. The shallow channel leads to the south bay of Whitefish. In summer we traverse it by canoe.

Approaching the lake, I could see one dim light on the mainland, one lamp of human presence. But darkness prevailed as I rounded the island. No "Starry Night" here. Usually I avoid darkness. I suppose most of us do. As a child I can remember my mother saying, "Come in when it gets dark." So we grow up keeping darkness at a distance. We learn to distrust it. It is a stranger whose secrets we fear. Yet every day of our lives it silently comes calling. But we pull the curtains, close the door and turn on the lights. We refuse to befriend it. Having turned the bend, I felt that familiar anxiety of childhood when you cannot see, when darkness seems so immense that you will get lost in it. I stopped. Surely my eyes would begin adjusting. But the lake's boundaries disappeared into infinite blackness. I had forgotten how much darker night is up here. Now I realize in Rochester, Minnesota, the sky is not black. The city's lights cast a mauve glow in the night softly illuminating our surroundings. Our perceptions have been altered, but we only know this when we enter such a night as this.

Gradually my pupils dilated. Gingerly I began walking. My confidence returned when I spotted deer tracks. Then I discerned the silhouettes of the trees bordering the island. Slowly I followed their comforting forms, certain I would find the channel. In summer thick reeds follow the island's shoreline and stop at the channel opening. But now only a few emerged from the snow-covered ice. So I walked looking up rather than down.

This night was as silent as the morning had been. But in darkness silence feels different. You are more alert. You listen and peer into the blackness with a greater intensity. Time changes. It loses definition with no visible markings to gauge progress. You become uncertain how long you have been walking. Very soon I became worried that I had been walking far too long, that I had passed the channel. I considered turning around and going back to the security of the cabin. But I could not give in now. I had come so far. I kept walking. Gradually I noticed more and more reeds. They brushed my legs with encouragement. Then abruptly they stopped. I had reached the opening! Two familiar trees towering over the others welcomed me. The channel spread out before me untouched. Its pristine mantle of snow invited me to walk through it. But I did not. I could not. I felt strangely compelled to preserve this sublime perfection as I had found it. It was the same sensation I experienced when I arrived   when I felt like an intruder. This place seemed like a sanctuary in the unbroken stillness. I perceived the channel as the nave of a cathedral. The trees bordering it were flying buttresses. The immaculate white lake beyond, the apse. I just stood immobile where I was in the narthex. There were no services tonight. No singing or chanting reached my ears. No prayers of comfort or supplication. Only this immense sanctuary of hallowed silence. I stood quietly musing. My thoughts wandered to the creation story, when "the earth was without form and void, and darkness was upon the face of the deep." I imagined the wonders of first light, the creation of the seas and lands, the sun, moon, and stars. I envisioned the world verdantly and newly alive with fishes, birds, and myriad creatures. And finally man and woman gracing this place of paradise. Then I recalled God's final observation in Genesis 1.31, "And God saw everything that he had made, and, behold it *was* very good."

It was then I walked through the channel. My snowshoe tracks declared I, too, belonged in this place. This sudden awareness, so intangible before, struck me like a clap of thunder. It illuminated my relationship to the landscape. Mine was not so much a mystical encounter as a spiritual revelation of my relationship to this earth. God considered his work good, and I was included in his assessment.

I shivered. Hugging myself I started back. My eyes, now fully adapted to the night, led me home with speed and certainty. I put on some water for a cup of tea.

MONDAY FEBRUARY 17

Arising an hour earlier this morning, I easily checked in with Byron by the appointed time. He cautioned me of the dangers I would face if the temperature plummeted. I smiled at his paternal concern. The thermometer registered a balmy 28°F.

Gray persists. The cloud covered sky above me is like a canopy. I am beginning to feel sequestered in a gigantic tent whose walls rise from the shoreline. My eyes search for the flaps, but none are visible. Snow fell last night from those heavy clouds holding their thousands of tiny waterdrops. And it looks as if more snow is coming. I suspect many droplets are now freezing around specks of dust high up there in the frigid air. Once I examined some snowflakes under a magnifying glass. My father had told me all of them would have six corners but none would be alike. He was right. Now these snowflakes are piled up from the wind, end to end, side by side, one on top of another. They have folded themselves into snowdrifts around the cabin. They have outlined in white every twig of every branch of every tree. Yesterday's snowshoe tracks are only memories. There is no indication of my presence here other than the woodsmoke hovering above the cabin. The island has undergone a complete restoration in the space of a night.

Walking toward the lake, I suddenly realized my water hole would be hidden as well. Never did it occur to me to mark it. But I was not about to auger another. I felt too dearly the pain of sore muscles from yesterday's efforts. Only one other choice was available   gathering snow. The task was simpler than I had imagined as the fresh snow was still loose. Using a cooking pot as a scoop, I filled two buckets. Then I heated more snow on the stove to hasten the melting and added the hot water to the packed buckets. The snow level fell to mere inches. Though it required many trips out the door and into the kitchen, the work was play compared to auguring and pumping.

I also needed wood. The porch woodpile was below screen level. Pulling a sled behind me, I snowshoed to the neighboring cabin where more wood was stored. Stacking the logs carefully, I was able to replenish the wood I had used in just two trips. I stoked the woodstove and carried in a supply of logs to last the day. My basic needs for water and warmth were now satisfied. I felt surprisingly invigorated from the morning's chores despite my sore muscles. Perhaps my middle aged body was getting into shape.

Warm from my labor, I sat on the porch swing gazing out at the white landscape. The snowbound earth. The frozen lake. The pale sky. This was a place erased of color. White memories began entering my mind. The loose flakes reminded me of the ivory ones my mother used to wash her lingerie, the sheets she loved hanging out in our backyard and how fresh they smelled that night on my bed. Then I thought of my grandmother's white hair rippling with crimps when she unbraided it at night. The fragile white magnolia blossoms I would carry home in summer. My mother would float them in a dish shaped like a swan. Their sweetness filled the entire house. I remembered my father's angelfood cakes and the airy morsels melting on my tongue. The milk toast and junket my mother served me when I was sick. Sand dollars drying on the porch railing at the beach. My wedding gown cascading behind me. Soft clean diapers. A freshly primed canvas. The tundra swans I spotted sleeping in the reeds last fall. A blank sheet of paper. The birch logs beside me now, their paper clothing fragmented and torn.

After lunch and a short rest, I was ready to go outside. I secured my snowshoes and walked down to the lake. No tracks were visible. Mine would be the first. As I walked, I found myself continually stopping and gazing back at my markings. Snowshoes make magnificent etchings in a herringbone design. It was absurd to be so taken with them, but I could not stop looking back. I thought their pattern was as remarkable as any creature's I had ever seen.

As I walked northwest, my attention turned to the third island. It lies beside the small one I passed on my arrival. At its crest is a cottage collapsed on itself from a fallen oak. This I discovered last summer when I canoed to the island. The cottage seemed so precarious then I feared entering it. Now I wished to check it again. In earlier years we could see the cottage whole and intact from the lake, but we never saw any signs of people.

In twenty minutes I was climbing the steep hill. Fallen trees, broken branches, and snarled underbrush forced me to remove my snowshoes. The snowcover was deep, but sinking in it was far more expedient than tripping and falling. The cottage soon came into view, its battered form coffined under a foot of snow. I began circling it slowly. Suddenly behind me I heard a huge beating in the air. Instinctively I turned, but too late. Whatever I stirred up flew into a camouflage of branches. All I could imagine was the great blue heron who nested on this island in summer. But he would not be here now. I was pleased, nevertheless. I had a neighbor.

In the backyard was the cast iron stove I remembered. It stood upright like a sentinel guarding the remains of another time. Why was the stove separate from the cottage? I wondered who removed it before the fatal storm which uprooted the oak. Turning, I spotted something aqua under the splintered roof. Coming closer I discovered plastic dishes with an aqua design. The cups reminded me of snow cones with their icy mounds.

I walked back to the front of the cottage. A triangular opening was created by the collapse, just large enough for me to get through. Should I? Yes. I determined the cottage had found its final form. Carefully I crawled in, keeping my head low. Soon I realized I could easily sit up in one area. The roof was at least four feet high. Surrounding me were the household's possessions. I had always imagined a trapper or woodsman living here alone – like Thoreau at Walden. But I was wrong. A family once called this home, for a hand made twig highchair had survived the debacle. Next to it was a bed crafted with tongue and groove planks. The pleasing curved headboard was bent willow. Its maker was a craftsman who placed importance on aesthetics. Next to the bed was its mate, crushed under the fallen roof. To my right was a broken table. Strewn around it was a sugar free Diet Rite cola, a cast iron skillet, a metal cooking pot, a battery, tin of pepper, and an empty can of Cherry Valley grapefruit juice. Crawling in deeper I found, under cruelly twisted planks, a rusted can of Raid Yard Guard and a first aid kit filled with dirt and mulched leaves. Too late for first aid here. I yearned to find a newspaper or a magazine. Anything with a date. Clearly a family had once lived here with their young child. Why did they leave? Why did they abandon all these possessions?

It is not for me to know why this family chose to live for a time on this remote island without water or electricity. They may have harbored an idealistic vision that went awry. Now their unexplained memory lingers in ruin and decay. Young saplings of pine and spruce surround this cottage. In their maturity they will conceal its existence; and in a greater space of time this place of abandonment will return to the soil. While walking through brush to the lake, I imagined a path worn smooth and familiar by this family's footsteps a path which recorded their story. Their coming and their going. What would they think if they returned today and encountered what I have seen? What memories would surge out of the snow draped planks? Musing about life's ongoing metamorphosis, I thought of some lines from *Milkweed*, a poem by James Wright.

"I look down now. It is all changed.
Whatever it was I lost, whatever I wept for
Was a wild, gentle thing... "

As I snowshoed back to our island, I knew the cabins there were also vulnerable. And I was vulnerable. Mortality stared at me so fixedly I could not blink it away. It occurred to me only the landscape will live on to watch life and death play out their eternal scripts. My sojourn here is brief. I own nothing. I can keep nothing. This place is simply on loan to me and my family for awhile. We are the temporary caretakers. Somehow our time on this planet seems inconsequential and as fleeting as tracks in the snow.

TUESDAY FEBRUARY 18

I slept fitfully, twice dreaming my mother died while visiting me. I awakened feeling disturbingly abandoned. Yet my mother is not my caretaker nor the focus of my life. Why such a feeling of despair? Perhaps mortality's intrusion yesterday affected me more than I realized. Perhaps I perceive the unconditional love in life is a mother's.

This unexpected melancholy lifted as Byron's cheerful voice answered my call. His "lecture" this morning concerned the bathroom heater. He was worried I might be leaving it on too long, and urged me to check the cord to see if it was hot   that heaters take more juice than lights and can be dangerous. I told him I had been using it sparingly but would check. It is comforting to know someone is concerned about me up here. Though these calls momentarily interrupt my solitude, I shall continue. I promised Tony and they give me surprising pleasure.

While dressing this morning I had a ridiculous accident. I was standing with my back to the woodstove and bent forward to change my underwear. Now I sport a fiery red streak across my buttocks. Solarcaine eased the burning but I appreciate the pillow now cushioning me.

Looking out the window I see the breadcrumbs I put out yesterday are untouched. It seems this place is still mine alone, though I now have the company of a westerly wind. The spruce boughs are swaying to its high whistling melody. I suspect a front is moving in. The sky still persists in its palette of gray, but its monotony is beginning to take on a soothing familiarity. In the four days I have been here, it is remarkable how empty and static this place has been. I have seen no creatures   only their signs in the snow and the sound of beating wings yesterday. Yet I am not lonely   perhaps because I chose to be here and know my time is limited. I am keenly aware my solitude can be terminated by lifting the phone. Unlike a life of solitude, my experience offers contrast and accessibility to human contact. Certainly the physical tasks of gathering wood and hauling in snow have been assets, despite my grumblings and misadventures. This necessary labor has provided focus and satisfaction and I have become stronger and confident. Furthermore, I have awaited each day with a sense of expectation unlike my scheduled and predictable life in Rochester.

I am beginning to see that solitude is not so much a physical state as a mental one, though coming here was the event which precipitated this perception. Unstructured time with no interruptions leads to introspection. The brain, lacking outward stimuli, surprisingly goes into high gear. Rarely does it stay in neutral. It travels in time zones. Yesterday, mine chose to go into reverse. It settled on the past event of my son's devastating illness, a drug induced psychosis. It was a time of painful self recriminations, a time of having to let go of all my expectations. I also remembered the wall of solitude which had encircled me. It was as intractable as stone, as immutable as the gray sky overhead. It was a solitude of profound aloneness. Solitude has that predilection whether it envelops us by choice or circumstance. The aloneness is self contained like an island. Ultimately we are isolated within ourselves. No one can truly enter into our psyches to know the pain or joy which resides there. In the end, I understood that solitude is the human condition.

So what is the point of seeking solitude if it is the essence of being human if I am as essentially alone at home as here at the island? I have unencumbered time. Time for reflection. Time to confront this solitary trait of being human.

This island solitude has indeed led to self discoveries some serious in nature, others frivolous. My behavior alone has astonished me. Unconstrained by society's mores, I have deliciously ignored personal etiquette and domestic responsibilities. My normal compunction for orderliness has deserted me. Clothes are heaped on the floor. Books, papers, and magazines are strewn about the cabin. Bread crumbs, limp teabags, and a knife streaked with marmalade leisurely wait on the kitchen counter. I have not combed my hair or put on make up. I am no longer changing clothes when I retire. I am disgustingly dirty. I am indulging in behavior which startles me. Yet I continue in this indulgence of uncivilized living because I know my civilized persona will re emerge when I re enter society.

A strange paradox has occurred however. My behavior in the landscape is the antithesis to that in the cabin. I am responding to the island and lake with respect, almost reverence. Each morning I have awakened to fresh snow. Perfection, if it exists, waits outside this cabin. When I enter it I still do so reluctantly, as I know my footprints will be the first to disturb its perfection. I am aware this is my habitat as well as the deer's, but I cannot enjoy those first steps. When I return from walking I always re trace my footprints to assure minimal altering of the snowcover. This behavior is unquestionably compulsive. I recognize this yet I have not changed my patterns. Perhaps because in the city the snow is soon shoveled, tramped on, and dirtied. Human imprints abound. Most are ugly.

A landscape image in Rochester is particularly haunting me. A river near my home has been devastated in the name of flood control. Monstrous machines have devoured eighty foot oaks and spit out their grotesque remains. This spring I will not see the river's borders of Virginia bluebells and phlox, or its trees of maple, poplar, and oak which supported abundant wildlife. Along the banks, graceful willows provided lodging materials to the beaver. Now all are gone. A sea of mud merges with snow where the machines stopped, creating a dark unsightly blemish. No wonder I am responding so compulsively to this sublime vista around me. This island seems like paradise. I suppose it has survived because our machines cannot get to it. I am beginning to understand John Muir's passionate efforts to create the national park system, after he went into the wilderness in the mid 1800's. There he called attention to its beauty and wildness. But we know the beauty he loved was not entirely safe.

Solitude has led to a second paradox beyond that of my behavior in and out of the cabin. In the paucity of stimuli solitude's absence has yielded fullness. I am immersed in a frenzy of words and images, accumulating even as I write. Continually I fear I shall forget what I have seen and thought. What absence looks like. What it feels like. What solitude encompasses.

These words are a beginning. Keeping a journal opens the blinds to one's interior landscape. While memory fails us, our writing endures. But the sense we employ most frequently to discover the world around us is seeing. Our eyes not only see shapes and colors but they also see the unseen and unspoken emotions communicated through gestures or facial expressions, or meanings through the use of symbols. At the precise moment the eyes see, the brain names and interprets the information. Our seeing becomes enmeshed with thought, with words. There appears to be a symbiotic relationship between images and words. We describe images with words; and likewise words create images in our consciousness. They are irrevocably connected. This connection is the frenzy embroiling me. Whatever I perceive metamorphoses into words and images, struggling for realization. Keeping a journal is my release for words, but I also need a visual release. For years I have made art. Much of it I have destroyed. Only recently did I submit work to juried shows. Both were willow pieces created with a friend, and their acceptance was most gratifying. Our collaboration has been a rich one, but there are pieces residing within me I long to create alone.

Five years ago I discovered wood. I love to touch it and run my fingers over its varied textures. Primarily I work with willow boughs cut in the landscape. They are tolerant and pliant and bend at will. Willow is smooth and gray in youth, becoming roughly textured and burnt umber as it matures. Often I juxtapose the two because it pleases me. The core is not porous, so it is strong and adaptable to the furniture which has been my primary focus in recent years. My tools are few. Loppers. Bow saw. Hammer. Drill. What has been most important to me is the journey   selecting the pieces in the willow grove, cutting them, hauling them out, and constructing them not always knowing where they will go. Before cutting, I sometimes visualize how a branch might appear in a chair, a folding screen, or a table. The variations offered by nature are limitless. Every tree has a story in its configuration   a curve speaks of seeking sunlight, a harsh angle of possible trauma. Scars may speak of a hungry deer. Mosses and lichen of moisture and decay. I have learned some trees are more suitable and interesting than others. Some are too large or too small. Others too gnarled or too straight. Their texture, size, or shape may suggest legs for a chair, a headboard for a bed, or seat pieces for a garden bench. I have discovered I cannot force the willow to conform with my vision. We must collaborate. When we collaborate, a piece works.

Artists are essentially vessels who fill themselves with sensory and emotional responses. Then they pour them out in their work. When I observed the cabin felled by the oak, I was filled with images of collapse and abandonment and loss. Intuitively I gathered some of the objects left behind. I visualized a construction in conjunction with these forlorn objects. This occurred within minutes of contemplating the shattered cabin. The image in my mind's eye continues to possess me, but experience has taught me the final work will be something else.

Tonight I enjoyed linguini with scallops and clams   another of my frozen dinners. It was far better than last night's bland lasagna. Each evening I have indulged in a glass of wine which I anticipate with much pleasure. I have marked the bottle with six strips of scotch tape to allow for a glass each day   another sign of my compulsive nature, I suppose. After dinner I took my coffee to the porch where the brisk air was as intoxicating as the wine. In the dark night I sat in the swing, listening to its creaking refrain.

My mother was resurrected in my dream last night. She strolled into my home and pulled out the roll away bed. Asking for linens, she made it up, carefully mitering the corners like she taught me as a child. Strangely I accepted her resurrection as quite natural, though I was most anxious that she not learn she had died. I suppose I thought she would be frightened. I remember gathering the newspaper and discarding it, while she picked up her purse that I fortunately had not moved. She never discovered she had lost a day. That was it. Then I awakened.

Mrs. Bromley answered the phone this morning. We have met only once, so are not on a first name basis. She promised to tell Byron I had called. I missed Byron's well meaning lecture and neighborliness.

The temperature has plummeted 18° and I am pleased. Cold enhances snowshoeing immeasurably. You do not sink down into mushiness, but stride the crunchy frozen surface. Again the infinite cloud cover is above me. If I were navigating by the heavenly bodies, I would have had to drop anchor long ago.

This morning I returned to the island's passage which leads to the back portion of the lake. I was curious to see this place in daylight. Within ten minutes I reached the passage prepared for any contingency, but nothing occurred. It was exquisitely lovely and still untouched, nothing more. Last night's snowflakes dusted the trees like fine sifted flour and softened their rigid silhouettes. I was injudicious to think I would enter a holy place again. I am beginning to question if we bring to nature or a landscape or anything else for that matter, a particular attitude. Do we unconsciously predispose what we will encounter? If we perceive a larger presence, will it be verified? I wonder if the overwhelming darkness of my first visit aroused my spiritual sensibilities because I was vulnerable. I felt awed by my insignificance and powerlessness in the black cold. Perhaps my mind was predisposed to perceive a greater power and the "cathedral" landscape fulfilled my unconscious expectations. This spiritual context thus yielded my insight of harmony and belonging. I was receptive and I received. It was not unlike the creative insight we are sometimes given. Both surface out of the unconscious. Neither can be sought consciously and purposefully.

I continued my walk along the south rim of the island passing a solitary rush curving eastward. Its tip was contained in the ice, creating a graceful arc. One sensed it was headed somewhere, so intent was its forward posture. I suspect the rush froze in a winter wind. It possessed the immobility of a gesture caught in a photograph. I stood transfixed by the poignancy of its solitude.

I proceeded to cross the island. It was difficult in my unwieldy snowshoes. Thickets and fallen trees were a continual challenge and I often stumbled. Heading west, I spotted the close footprints of a rabbit, walking like I was. Soon I reached a point where the prints formed a circle. Then I came upon two sets of prints side by side. Apparently two rabbits had met one another and proceeded on together. Somehow this simple encounter gave me great pleasure. Perhaps because I had discovered neighbors I imagined as friendly. I suspect solitude amplifies the loss of community and this encounter revealed its importance to me. This could also explain my pleasure in speaking with Byron each morning.

I continued walking west expecting to reach Birchwood cabin or the bunkhouse just beyond it. Soon I spotted the familiar tobacco brown. Moving closer I was startled to discover I was at Homestead Cabin, which is east! How could I have been so disoriented? But then, why should I presume I would not get confused with no recognizable boundaries in the woods' midst? I must bring a compass on my next visit.

It is 10:30 pm. I glance at the clock in the kitchen now and then to see how my biological clock compares to my cycles back home. They have been surprisingly similar. It seems our habits have a tenacious grip on us.

Solitude I have found to be a fine companion. The days are mine to live as I choose. What has astonished me is time. When I awaken free of any agendas, it seems limitless. Yet the clock informs me that it races. I believe this phenomenon is due to the extraordinary circumstances I have placed myself in.

In my "civilized" life there are the same routines and expectations which present themselves day after day. I always have tomorrow to accomplish them. I do not sense time's fleeting nature.

The difference here in this "wilderness" landscape is I am continually aware I have only seven days to choose how I will live. I want to glean all that I can from each hour of each day. I value my time because it holds possibility and discovery. There are no familiar expectations to lull me into automatic behavior. No beds to make. No laundry to wash. No pets to feed. No children and husband to placate. No sameness. So who am I alone? How have I lived? I am a woman, awake and productive. I have made decisions and acted on them. I have gathered wood and secured water for survival. I have photographed the landscape and snowshoed its length and breadth. I have listened to silence. I have mused and dreamed. I have been consumed with ideas which I jot down on coffee filters, grocery bags, and paper towels. Through my writing I am beginning to perceive the texture of my interior landscape as well as that of the exterior one. This solitude has permitted me to escape from the chrysalis of dormancy which too often snares me at home. I am flying. I am seeing and hearing. I am feeling and thinking. I am fully conscious of my living.

Byron and I talked about the dangers of contaminated snow this morning. He urged me to boil any snow I melted. It is difficult to imagine this lovely fresh snow might not be safe. But I shall heed his advice.

The wind is roaring today, challenging the old Reeves stove to keep me warm. Last night I did not awaken at 3 am to stoke the stove, so it is starting from a bed of cold ashes. Already my coffee is cold. I am sitting close to the stove trying to evade the drafts coming in the east windows. I suppose I could crawl back into my sleeping bag, but I am too fully awake. This is the first day I am cold. The difference is the wind. I am now grateful for the stillness of the past five days.

Yesterday afternoon I indulged in a nap by the stove where I now sit. It elicited my one memory of being here one cold winter day. Tony and I had driven up to snowshoe and have a picnic. Reaching the cabin we heaped wood into the stove and heated seafood chowder purchased at Morey's Fish House on the drive up. The rich steaming chowder was delicious after our hike across the lake, but the cabin was cold. It would be hours before the stove could make it comfortable. Impulsively I went to the back bedroom, grabbed Tony's sleeping bag and spread it by the stove, undressed, and slipped into the soft down. Tony was stunned at my unexpected invitation. Grinning, he too undressed and joined me in our cocoon of pleasure. Our lovemaking has rarely exceeded the rush of that cold afternoon. Ordinary circumstances prohibit such sweet abandon. Too often we are tired or preoccupied. At home are the distractions of children, telephones, and pets. None respect private passion on a Saturday afternoon.

After dinner last night I fell into a languorous mood, unable to muster enough energy to even read. I draped myself over the easy chair and thumbed mindlessly through magazines left here through the years. The mood did not dissipate until close to ten. Then my energy somehow reinvented itself. I felt ebullient and incredibly carefree. I began loudly singing, "Good morning, Mr. Zip Zip Zip" and other songs from my childhood. Impetuously, I stood on my head, touched my toes, and did a cartwheel. I conversed with the cracking logs and let out a glorious scream. I even belched with abandon. I have never behaved quite like this before, yet I could not have been intoxicated from one glass of wine at dinner. My behavior was like a Dada performance. Unpredictable. Absurd. Obscenely delicious. What was I reacting to? Cabin fever? The proprieties of society? Or was I tripping into insanity?

I have just finished May Sarton's *Journal of a Solitude* which I cannot dismiss from my mind; for Sarton described what I suddenly understood only a few days ago. She wrote, "When it comes to the important things, one is always alone. The way one handles this absolute aloneness... is the great psychic journey of everyman." I suppose this solitary "psychic journey" is one we all confront at some point in our lives. My physical solitude here has illuminated its truth for me. Memories have returned and confirmed Sarton's insight. My marriage. The births of my children. David's devastating illness... I *was* alone in these times. I have found this a disquieting realization to accept. It is a profoundly empty feeling to surrender to the knowledge of one's ultimate aloneness.

Physical solitude has been far simpler to confront and endure. Aloneness in this landscape has acted like an elixir and been a marvelous panacea physically. When I snowshoed today I felt particularly invigorated. I waited until the wind died down. The air was a frosty 11°. I inhaled deeply. Having been inside all day, the rush of air in my lungs was cool and delicious. I held on to its fragrance of firs and spruce, its reassuring aroma of woodsmoke. I began walking and headed for the end of the island where I mistakenly thought I was yesterday. Following the shoreline to its tip, I then searched for a deer trail to follow. I continue to trust their judgment in these matters and was not let down. The trail was clear and manageable. Like the deer, I walked quietly and confidently. I am stronger now. Hills no longer convert my heart to a pounding drum. I think this snowshoeing has shed a decade from my middle aged body.

The woods were still silent this afternoon. As I walked I felt inextricably woven into the fabric of this solitary island as surely as the unseen creatures about me.

As I breakfasted this morning beside the freshly stoked woodstove, it occurred to me how entirely comfortable I felt. Over the course of these seven days my presence has filled this cabin and the landscape out my window. Routines are established and familiar. There is a measure of self reliance in all I undertake. I am a full fledged member of the neighborhood.

Tomorrow I return to Rochester. To my home. To my family. Their images are beginning to fill my consciousness. It will be good to enter their lives again, but I shall miss this place of silence. It has served me well and nurtured my capacity to live more fully. The landscape has played the protagonist these seven days with unceasing fervor. It has riveted my senses and raised my consciousness.

As I write, I wonder if I have given proper shape to this drama of silence and my participation in it. Some writers believe we should write from a distance of time, that our immediate perceptions can be faulty. In the months to come I may well reassess what I have recorded, but for now this is how it was as I lived it.

I have discovered solitude on an island juxtaposes the exterior world of color and texture against that of the interior landscape. I have confronted silence and absence and found fullness. I have challenged this cold harsh landscape and found self reliance. I have observed the disappearance of boundaries, yet felt encircled by the perpetual grey sky I perceive as a grand minimalist shelter. In the darkness of night I discovered a spiritual sensibility. In returning from the cold, I experienced the pleasure of warmth. In the absence of human companionship, I befriended myself. However, lack of water for bathing I am finding almost unendurable!

I took to the road last Saturday with the destination Paradise. If the Greeks' Elysian Fields are paradise I did not find it, as this island is no land of "song and sunlight," green meadows, or flowers. If paradise is the Islamic dream of a verdant oasis with plenty of water, I did not find it. If paradise is Dean's and Sal's dream of excitement and movement, I did not find it. If paradise is the place where God's immediate presence is felt, a door has been cracked. If paradise is a heightened capacity to live, I am sitting in heaven.

SPRING

Exterior

SATURDAY MAY 16

Today Spring and I departed together for the island. As I pulled out of the driveway, I inhaled her fragrant lilacs and watched the Baltimore orioles feasting on the fruit of the horse chestnut trees. Lush green was underfoot and overhead. Through Minneapolis, St. Cloud, Little Falls, and Motley, Spring was beside me with her green paintbrush. But when I reached Ackley, her greens were sparer and thinner. Drybrushed. She seemed reluctant, as if yearning to linger in the warmer landscape behind us. Doggedly I drove on. When I turned onto the dirt road leading to Whitefish Lake, she was only tentatively greening the earth. I arrived before she was fully present. The quaking aspen leaves were no larger than nickels. Pale green grasses were struggling through the brown leaf remnants of last autumn. Woodland ferns were still curled into their fetal postures, whereas those at home were as high as my knees, their fronds spread wide.

A gentle rain was falling when I pulled into Byron Bromley's driveway a half mile from our lake. Winter's gray sky greeted me like an old friend. Byron and I had arranged to meet, as I needed his assistance to launch the bass boat, pull out the island dock, and reassemble the plumbing. He greeted me with a great hug, then followed me in his truck to the landing. We easily slid the boat over the slick grass in short bursts of effort. The rain was an unexpected pair of hands. I unloaded my gear while Byron attached the Yamaha motor. A portion of our ancient dock was submerged, its posts leaning haphazardly with no footings left after the long winter. "Only Tuesday a week ago the ice left the lake," Byron told me. The thaw must have been the final assault.

Moments after we started across the lake, the great blue heron swept by in welcome. His long slender legs trailed gracefully behind him like those of a diver. I smiled and watched his familiar glide just below tree level. I wondered if the loons had returned, too, for I had never come up here this early in spring. I longed to hear their laughter across the lake, their plaintive voices at night. Nearing the island I cut the motor and we gently drifted into the bank. I tied the boat to a nearby sapling and we carried my provisions to the cabin.

After turning on the electricity and gas, Byron and I hauled water to the pumphouse to prime the pump. Within a few minutes the gauge reached 40 pounds of pressure and the pump cut off. Entering the cabin, we heard a thunderous sound emanating from the bathroom. My husband had unhooked the washer hoses.

Byron sped outside to turn off the water while I frantically tried to catch the gush in two plastic cups I spotted on the sink. In no time the water was off and we reattached the hoses. The bathroom rug was saturated. Once more Byron turned on the water. Then I walked into the kitchen. Water was seeping from under the sink.

I opened the cabinet doors and fell back as water squirted in my face. Again Tony surprised us in his thoroughness. He had removed a bleeding valve cap. Byron was already running to the pumphouse, as I feebly attempted to find a container. Shivering and wet I began emptying the cabinet of its soggy paper towels, household cleaners, dish rack, and a bag of tiles.

The bag broke scattering the tiles on the wet muddy floor. Byron and I began searching through the mess for the missing valve cap. Defeated, I called Tony. He had taped it on the cabinet near the bathroom. Byron reattached it and turned on the water for the last time. Our first project was finished except for the alarming mess in the kitchen which Byron did not seem to notice as he strode toward the dock.

Immediately, Byron informed me the tires which support and roll the dock into the lake were flat. He said we would have to drive to Blackduck to have them repaired. My spirits sank. I had imagined I would soon be boating him back to the mainland and solitude would be mine. Then he casually mentioned we could eat dinner there, that he knew a "really good" restaurant and would like to "treat." I knew I was defeated. What I did not know was this saga would last six hours.

Fortunately, Blackduck is only sixteen miles away. As we drove through greening farmlands Byron acted as a tour guide, pointing out which farms had "gone under" and the "longest driveway in Minnesota." Shortly I pulled into the Conoco station. Byron talked to a teenaged boy about the tires, while I filled two empty gas cans which I had spotted before leaving. Thirty minutes later the tires were ready and I paid the bill. Only $14.88.

Byron gestured toward a parking place in the next block. I pulled in and we crossed the street to Trail's End Restaurant. It was now 7:30 pm. I had arrived at Byron's four hours ago. The room was empty except for three high school girls drinking Pepsi's. Byron ushered me to a table commenting how he loved this restaurant. He liked its "homeyness and good food" and asked me if I liked the antiques. I looked around, slightly flustered, as I saw none. Then I noticed, hanging on the knotty pine walls, antique logging and farming tools.

Smiling, I said, "Yes, that's a wonderful collection." Beaming, Byron pointed out the various implements and carefully explained their uses.

Garrison Keillor would approve of this place. Hot grease wafted from the kitchen. Cheerful blue and white polka dot oil cloths covered the tables. Underfoot was a patchwork print carpet and overhead faded plastic ferns. The only waitress brought us laminated menus and tepid water in scratched plastic glasses. I scanned the list of sandwiches and asked Byron which he recommended. "I've brought you here for dinner, not a sandwich," he admonished with a wink. I chose fish, baked potato, and slaw. Byron then quipped, "I'll have the same as the lady," and asked for a pot of coffee. As Byron filled my cup, I asked him about his family and how he liked living up here. Soon our food arrived. The fish tasted frozen, but I ate it all. I was hungrier than I realized.

We both declined desert and I thanked him for the dinner. It was growing dark as we unloaded the tires and gas cans at the island. Byron installed the tires as he directed me to lift the supports. With the strength of Paul Bunyan, he heaved the dock into the lake. It rolled out perfectly. I waded into the water to help him stabilize it, grateful I had on my knee high Fleet Farm boots.

We climbed into the bass boat and I motored him back to the mainland. It was 9:45 pm and the night was black. Fortunately, I know the lake intimately, and easily made it back. As I walked toward the cabin I let out a lusty cheer. I was finally alone.

Entering the cabin, I remembered the mess in the kitchen. Besieged with the identity of Mrs. Clean, I mopped the floor, wiped down the cabinets and counters, vacuumed the dried mud in the living room and swept the porch. I had not yet shed my "civilized" housekeeping compulsions. I needed to begin the week with order, even though I knew it would not last. My behavior was familiar to me. When I begin a project, I need orderly surroundings. Then I can cook or write or make art. Though my process always yields to chaos, this never disturbs me. Somehow the work supersedes my Mrs. Clean identity.

The phone rang as I was underway. It was Byron checking to see if I had gotten back safely. He is such a dear thoughtful man, but today's long saga frustrated me. I was impatient for solitude. I suppose Byron's needs were the opposite. With his quiet routines, these hours of helping me and treating me to a dinner must have been a refreshing change.

At 12:30 am I wearily slipped into bed, thinking how different my spring arrival was from winter's. Today I was dependent on another human being. Why do I find this so unsettling? Perhaps I long to be free of needing others   to prove to myself and the world I am independent and self sufficient. Or did these desires arise because I am a woman attempting to find "a room of my own"?

Solitude has a different character this visit. The cold white majesty and silence of winter has been transformed into the sweet refrains of spring. This morning bird song awakened me as sunlight airbrushed window patterns on the wall. Eagerly I arose, and after a hurried breakfast of coffee and an English muffin I laid a fire. The air was a chilly 40°. I walked down to the lake. Two loons were leisurely swimming and conversing in the distance. It seems we think of loons as certifying solitude. But today there was a sense of community. My former perception of solitude as absence disappeared in a landscape filled with sound and light.

I headed for the path which leads to Birchwood Cabin. On both sides of me yellow, white, and lavender glimmered like gemstones. Bellworts by the hundreds bowed their heads while tiny white wood anemones and woodland violets raised theirs. I began gathering a bouquet and memories of other springs surged through me. Springs of childhood offerings limp upon their presentation to my mother. Springs when my own daughter, Molly, presented me with her gift of flowers.

I gazed upward. Doilies of young foliage were etching the azure sky. Quaking aspens whispered to me, coaxing me into their midst. I left the path. The woods were still clear cut from winter, though petite ferns and spring green grasses were peeking ·through the moist soil and mulched leaves. Soon I came upon pussytoes and dandelions in a clearing. Then I spotted two jack in the pulpits and one solitary trillium. Spring had made greater headway than I had perceived yesterday. Somewhere ahead of me I heard two tapping sounds, one light the other deep and resonate. Following them I spotted what I thought was a downy woodpecker, but later I discovered in Peterson's field guide it was a yellow bellied sapsucker.

I marveled at the remarkably parallel rows of holes he had drilled in search of insects and sap. I walked on attempting to locate the deeper intermittent tapping. Nearing Homestead cabin I stopped to listen once more. The tapping resumed high above me. Looking up I spotted a magnificent pileated woodpecker. Within moments beating wings lifted him out of sight. I had seen one only once before, but there was no doubt about his identity. He was as large as a crow and flashed black and white under his brilliant red crest. Exhilarated, I mused about spring's capacity to raise our spirits, to connect us to the marvels of nature. The morning's sweetness was so intense that I suddenly sensed its fleeting nature, and a melancholy enveloped me. Unexpectedly I knew someday I would know my last spring. Just like I would know other last things in my life. The last sight of a friend or loved one. The last time to make love, the last time to hear my name spoken. Fortunately, we rarely know these are last moments. I suspect even those dying believe they will feel the touch of a human hand once more. Perhaps this simple faith is how we should perceive each spring given to us. But my greatest consolation is spring's eternal reincarnation. The newborn yellows, lavenders, and greens now bursting forth will return for generations to come.

I made my way back to the cabin. I decided to write awhile, but after describing my morning walk, I had nothing more to say. Doodles and scribblings began filling the margins of my journal. I soon recognized I was going nowhere. Restless, I went outside to enjoy the sunshine. Grabbing a blanket, I spread it on the grass behind the cabin. I lay down. The sun rapidly warmed and relaxed me. Knowing I had perfect privacy, I removed my jeans and shirt. Exquisitely free, I lay on my stomach under the sun's brilliant rays, watching the bees and butterflies dart among the dandelions and pussytoes in unencumbered freedom. We were all partaking the gifts spring offered. We needed nothing. We were in Eden. I dozed off.

Late afternoon ushered in a cool wind. Buttoning my shirt I came inside. The morning fire I had laid was cold, but the cabin still held its warmth. I mused about the day as I started supper. I had accomplished nothing in terms of producing something tangible, but surprisingly I was not assaulted by guilt. I felt renewed and at peace. I had inhaled spring and permitted her to enter my soul and nourish my body.

My peace was interrupted, however, as I sipped coffee after dinner. I felt something move on my back. It was a tick. Over the next hour I discovered seven more. Generally ticks do not particularly bother me, but tonight's influx unnerved me. On the kitchen sink is a pile of matches   a funeral pyre for the lives I have snuffed out. It seems my early walk in the woods was not just about spring's lovely gifts.

At 10:30 pm I slid into my sleeping bag. Just now I felt something crawling on my thigh. I am back in the kitchen. The ninth tick has felt the fire of my dismay. I cannot stop brooding about them, and am imagining more crawling when none are there. I am profoundly uneasy and weary. Sweet sleep, come visit me.

MONDAY MAY 18

Sunlight awakened me again. It illuminated the shapes of the window panes on the wall across the room. I lay awhile watching the reflections slowly move as the sun rose in the sky. Today was brilliant, though still a cool 50°. I slipped into my sweatsuit and brewed a pot of coffee. The matches from last night were waiting on the sink. After discarding them, my tick nightmare gradually receded. I discovered no more. When I return to the woods I shall cover myself completely.

Spring has intensified from yesterday's warmth. The ferns seem to have doubled in size. They must be eight inches high! The trees are denser, the grass visibly greener. Green permeates the landscape, coloring its roof and floor. I thought of Picasso talking with Christian Zervos in *The Creative Process*. Picasso spoke of walking in the forest of Fontainbleu, getting "an indigestion of greenness" which he needed to "empty into a picture". In this conversation Zervos was interviewing Picasso about his creative process. I also recall Picasso talked about art as intensively as he made it. Painting was his life. A dimension of his very being. Ultimately the conversation revealed Picasso valued who was inside the artist more than what he created. He was intensely scornful of people, particularly critics, who attempt to understand painting when "there is no attempt to understand the "song of birds... " or to "love a flower." For Picasso, those who attempted to find meaning in art were on the wrong track. It was simply to be experienced.

Picasso's disdain for seeking meaning in art disturbs me. I work in a gallery where I have witnessed the richness of the aesthetic response as well as the poverty of the disinterested one. The aesthetic response not only strikes an emotional chord in the viewer, but also challenges the intellect to understand the work. I have been "guilty" of dialogues with some of our clients. Together we have sought meaning in works in the gallery. These dialogues have been rich and enlightening, even though I acknowledge our interpretations are inconclusive. I am unquestionably at odds with Picasso.

Many of us have observed others immersed in a magnificent piece of theatre or spellbound by a work of art. I well remember observing my mother losing herself in music and my daughter doing the same in poetry. I remember discovering in Mark Rothko's canvases that art can change one's concept of time and yield new perceptions of the sublime.

Without question, great music, literature, and painting, as well as nature's canvases, have the power to capture us. Challenge us. Engage us. When an aesthetic experience occurs we feel uplifted. Our senses are heightened. The arts provide a world where our horizons are broadened by connecting us to people in other times and other places. There are moments when it can present us with visions which compel us to explore our own minds and experiences. Anne Sheppard in *Aesthetics* also spoke to this experience when she wrote, "However good our standard of living, however perfect our social arrangements, however upright our way of life, our lives will be poorer and more limited if we lack opportunities for aesthetic appreciation."

Later this afternoon I went back to the woods. Well covered. While wandering in the west end of the island, I happened upon two abandoned structures I had not seen before. The larger was a flattened mass of rotting planks, broken doors, and shattered windows. It occurred to me it might be the fifth cabin which once existed, though my family has always believed another area of timbers is its location. The second smaller structure was leaning severely. Planks were broken and missing. Others were decaying. But its sharply angled form possessed a surprising grace. The missing planks revealed its vulnerability and mortality. Pale green lichens were strewn across it like spattered paint. The structure, enclosed by mosses and vines, suggested a sarcophagus.

I walked back to the cabin thinking about this forlorn structure which had fallen in on itself something like the cabin I visited in winter. Paradoxes surfaced into my consciousness. The structure was coarse, yet elegant. Dead, yet yielded life. Transparent, yet closed. In my mind's eye a vision began focusing. I could not dismiss its power over me. I began perceiving a work speaking to collapse and abandonment, to loss and renewal.

My resolve was clear. I would return to dismantle this structure only to build another. This, too, would be collapsed. I believed the process would reveal perpetual creation and irretrievable loss. Immediately I returned to the tool shed to get my hammer. Soon I was removing hundreds of rusty nails. The planks beside me grew into jagged stacks of gray. Two hours later I began transporting the planks to the lake's edge. The hill leading to the shore was steep and thick with brush. It required numerous descents before I finished. After supper I canoed to the waiting planks and piled them across the canoe's thwarts. Paddling back slowly with my unwieldy load, I eagerly anticipated the work ahead.

TUESDAY MAY 19

The familiar chorus of birdsong aroused me at 7:30 am. Again the sunny windowpanes were slow dancing across the wall. I have discovered I can tell the time by their position.

After coffee and an English muffin with marmalade, I walked to Birchwood Cabin. The morning sun would be right to photograph the birch grove beside it. Nearing the cabin I spotted a reddish brown blur disappear under the foundation. "Hello, come out," I called. To my amazement, a young fox obediently sauntered out. Our eyes met. We stared at each other perhaps ten seconds. Then he ambled back into the darkness. He did not seem to find me threatening. But for a split second I wondered if I were in danger. I only know this wild creature from literature and zoos, and "docile" is not a trait I have associated with the fox. But my anxiety was unfounded. His gaze had not been threatening. Simply questioning. And why not? I was the visitor.

Elated with my encounter, I skipped back to the cabin laughing at my moment of foolish fear. I was so delighted with my new neighbor I twirled with the aspen leaves billowing about me. This simple creature had raised me up like a sail. But why was I so elated? I am not conscious that I am lonely, yet my joy was astonishing. Perhaps I have been denying a need for companionship   even that of a wild creature. Somehow those inquiring eyes looking into mine affirmed my existence. Without question that little fox engaged me. I forgot to photograph the birches.

Back at Homestead cabin I wrote awhile before lunching on a lettuce and tomato sandwich. Eager to begin my construction, I gathered my bow saw, hammer, and nails. The sun was playing hide and seek in the clouds as I made my preparations. It was a fine day to be outside. Near the dock, the weathered planks waited with their blackened nail holes. I looked at them, suddenly uncertain how I should begin. My mind's image had not supplied the details.

Tentatively, I began the work by constructing a frame with the 2x4's I had salvaged. I laid them on the grass like a flattened box to orient myself, then nailed one side at a time. I used only one nail at each juncture so the structure would be flexible. This was so successful that as I nailed later sides, the piece almost collapsed. Hand sawing the jagged planks was the next step. It was not long before my arm ached with fatigue. I had no gloves and soon found I was bleeding from nicks. In time a blister formed in the fleshy area between my thumb and first finger. But I could not stop and risk bad weather. I nailed the planks to the frame in the uneven fashion I found them. Then I realized I was running short. There were no more planks to salvage. My solution was leaving the door and roof open. It worked. Thirsty, I walked up to Homestead cabin for water, and discovered five hours had passed. Time had ceased to exist. But in the space of an afternoon, a palpable form rose up by the shore. It arose out of an experience, an idea and a vision. Its scale is smaller than I envisioned, but its character is all I had hoped it would be.

I am bone weary tonight, but satisfied. I had forgotten how much energy making art demands.

WEDNESDAY MAY 20

Island solitude is being redefined in this season of spring. Trilling, tapping and swooping, crawling, creeping and growing abound. A devoted rough winged swallow has made her nest under the cabin's eaves. Each time I leave the cabin I fear I alarm her, as she heads for the nearby fir. She intently watches for my certain departure before returning to her young. Observing her in the warm morning air, I decided to breakfast on the porch. While eating, a great blur of red and black skimmed by. It was the spectacular pileated woodpecker. Shortly afterwards, I observed two plump robins stalking worms in the warm earth and a gray squirrel cautiously surveying the landscape. We were all serenaded by the rhythmic tapping of the yellow bellied sapsucker and distant loons calling to their mates.

After breakfast this morning I went back to Birchwood Cabin to photograph the nearby birches. To my amazement, my new neighbor, the fox, came out to greet me with his steady curious gaze. I wished him "good morning." Immensely pleased, I proceeded to the birch grove and made my photographs.

Throughout the day sunshine saturated the air. By late morning I again succumbed to the sun's warmth. Lying on the grass I lazily watched the honeybees feasting among the pussytoes. Butterflies I could not name joined in the search of the flowers' sweet nectar, while inches from my face tiny ebony ants climbed up and down the countless blades of grass. I pondered what their destination might be. Their work seemed so entirely futile, yet I suppose my labors yesterday might be construed in the same way. Even a ruby throated hummingbird joined the workforce. In the brilliant sunlight, it gleamed like a ruby and emerald set in motion. The profuse life surrounding me suggested an immense Jackson Pollack canvas, an "action painting" of dynamic vitality. It teemed with energy, flinging and dripping color and movement about me. It drew me into its rhythms and complex webbing. I was inextricably entangled in its effervescent gestures. Alive.

This evening I went for a canoe ride. The first dragonflies of the season had just arrived. Chasing mosquitoes they agilely performed acrobatic feats challenging the great Wallendaas   flying in circles, suddenly dropping low, then dancing off into the sky where I lost them. And off the canoe's bow, hundreds, perhaps thousands of minute flying insects moved in a cloud of their own making.

Now darkness prevails. On the screen beside me, seven glistening May beetles (June bugs in June) tenaciously cling, drawn to the light from the kitchen. My species on this island is greatly outnumbered.

But they are ever present... Today each of my children called. Molly, to test my reaction to her proposal to resign her job and come here for the summer. I asked her what she was planning to do. Her vague answer suggested she was wishing to escape the complexities of her life. My answer was "no." David called to see how I was doing and if I were lonely. I simply described my surroundings. And Paul called to wish me a belated "Happy Mother's Day." He was out of town at the time and felt badly that he had not thought ahead to leave me a card. He promised me a fishing rod. I told him I would love one.

Then my husband got on the line. I humorously related my misadventures with Byron on my arrival and our dinner in Blackduck, but he saw no humor whatever. In fact he felt threatened, and commented that people might be interpreting my solitary trips as a symptom of a disintegrating marriage. I was stunned. I knew the friends I told of my experiment believed me. But it struck me he was genuinely concerned.

My husband's reaction upset me. Since my arrival, the landscape and then my collapsed structure have been so consuming I have given little thought to my family or my marriage. But tonight I cannot dismiss what his call has led me to confront and remember. In the past few years I am aware I have been distancing my dependency on Tony and on my children. It began with David's terrifying illness and later Molly's struggles to finish her college work at Barnard. She had been considering quitting with only a semester to go. When my husband plunged into despair I realized my primary sources of security and fulfillment were faltering. To keep myself afloat, I had to sever my dependency on my family and look within myself.

Having married quite young, my notions of marriage were embarrassingly naive. I looked to my husband to meet my emotional needs. To provide for me. To be strong and invulnerable. To replace my father. I did not perceive I too could equally shoulder marriage's responsibilities. Then I discovered a dependent relationship was a vulnerable one. It carried no warranty. It was urgent that I redefine my expectations. About to withdraw from graduate school, I continued despite the family's ordeals. I looked within myself and found unsuspected reserves. I turned to other women and found wisdom and strength.

Tonight inside this cabin, I am also inside my psyche, seeking answers about my marriage and my "self." I think my husband is sensing the changes in me and is struggling to interpret them. But I shall not return to my former dependency. Marriage must be a loving union of two self sufficient people. Dependent relationships only stifle growth and lead to insecurity. It is unfortunate that it often takes trauma's intrusion to illuminate such truths. I go forward now secure in my capability to survive. Secure in my capability to contribute. I am especially grateful these solitary island visits entered my life. They have offered a format for further reflection. Solitude, it seems, is a catalyst for not only confronting one's outer landscape, but also one's interior one. Like winter, it clear cuts the undergrowth and opens new passages for self realization.

For two consecutive days the thermometer has risen to 80°. The delicious warmth has brought me outside most of each day, and my formerly pale body is rapidly browning. I often wait until darkness to write and I sense a clear difference in the content from my last visit. I seem to be focusing more on activity than reflection, outwardness more than inwardness. In part it is the allure and accessibility of the landscape. Today it is warmer outside than in the cabin. But also I have felt distinctly different. I have been more restless. I constantly go outside as if I am searching for something, but I do not know what it is. There is not the profound quiet to quiet me.

Today I mowed. The grass was rapidly growing out of control. After some five hours of labor I hauled the complaining mower into the shed. Around the cabins the fuzz of mowed pussytoes hugged the ground like lint. The trim lawn now speaks to human presence. I like to think I have harnessed spring's wild energies for a while, particularly the mosquitoes which thrive if we allow the grass to grow too long. Or did my normal compulsion for neatness play itself out in my mowing marathon? I cannot deny I find deep satisfaction in seeing the grass around the cabins "civilized." Whenever it is overgrown I feel the place looks rundown and neglected. My family has designated me the official mower. They made a wise choice.

Spring's landscape, unlike winter's, closes in. The southern sky is invisible through the trees. The island feels more like the mainland. Deer trails are now camouflaged by new growth. In the brief time I have been here the woods have thickened with foliage too dense to negotiate. Only the path to Birchwood Cabin permits passage. I inhabit a landscape of boundaries. There is no longer a question of where one ends and the other begins.

Before coming on this trip, I packed the photographs I took this winter. It occurred to me that it would be interesting to re photograph this landscape from the precise vantage points I chose last February. The task has been formidable and revealing. I discovered there are photographs I made while standing on the lake, which alerted me again to the limitations of my present boundaries. Since I cannot walk on water I launched the canoe, but the lake did not respond to my command to be still. As soon as I would frame a picture, a wave would gently lap the canoe, framing its own.

I have been re-reading my winter writings each evening. Distancing oneself for a period of time re-focuses one's memories and impressions. The reading has revealed images only partially formed in winter. Now I am perceiving pieces I wish to construct. I think this retrospective exercise points to what was most authentic from that sojourn. I shall re-read these pages again in the future to test my hypothesis.

My spring pilgrimage has yielded the reconstructed shelter now residing by the dock. I credit solitude's freedom from responsibilities for its existence. Today I sat across from my impoverished assemblage, contemplating its form and its textures, its melancholy. I realized again I know no more about its origins than the collapsed cabin I visited last winter. The two are indubitably connected. Suddenly I felt compelled to return. I needed to see it once more. Were the questions it raised then still valid? Would its mystery still engage me in this new season? Would its lost memories and vulnerability still speak to me? I went back to look. Now the cabin rests in a snarled tangle of grasses and weeds, not a coffin of white crystals. Its musty dark cavity sheltering the family's belongings still speaks to their mysterious departure. The profuse undergrowth articulates a feeling of abandonment more poignant than I remembered. I recognized my small shelter seemed powerless compared to this cabin. But even though its scale lacks power, I believe that its form and texture are honest reflections of what I saw and felt. Time did its worst to the island cabin and that which I dismantled, but in doing so the results seem timeless.

Spring's warmth has gone elsewhere. This morning's forty degree temperature sent me deep into my sleeping bag. Rain fell all night and continued most of today. I slept until 8:30 am with no sun streaming in or birdsong to awaken me. It was to be a day spent indoors. Only twenty four hours ago I was certain the old Reeves woodstove had fulfilled its contract. But today I was forced to renew it. Fortunately the stove acquiesced.

Most of the day I spent reading and writing. All my pencils have grown dull, so I am sharpening them with a carving knife from the kitchen drawer. My typist has been urging me to use a word processor or computer that the hours I spend re writing by hand would be freed for other pursuits. She is undoubtedly right. But I lamely resist. All the labeled keys and functions engage my attention and I worry about making mistakes. I feel so frustrated about the act of typing that words falter. I become immobilized. Perhaps I have not given technology enough time, but in all honesty, I am intimidated by this computer age. I still prefer watches and clocks with hands, televisions and radios with knobs, and writing implements with graphite. The only defense I have discovered for continuing to write by hand was an article I read about the author, Alexander Solzhenitsyn. He writes all his manuscripts in longhand!

Late this afternoon the rain abated and I grabbed the opportunity to go outside. I still had some photographs I wished to take and was anxious to escape the cabin's confinement. The island was eerily quiet. No chirping. No buzzing. No creatures. I assumed they were still in their nests and shelters. I took just a few photographs my reconstruction, the depleted woodpile, and a mangled tree which caught my attention. The woods were so wet, water trickled down my neck and my Keds squished as I walked. No matter, the dry cabin waited to warm and shelter me.

This second visit is almost over. I depart for home tomorrow. It has been another satisfying experience, though far different from my first. Spring solitude has not possessed the profundity I experienced in winter. Until today, unceasing sound and activity surrounded me. A sense of community has prevailed   not the absence and silence of February. Though I heard human voices only on the day my family called, I have not been lonely. Solitude and I are quite compatible and have remained on good terms now for fourteen days. Recently a friend wrote that she could not imagine my managing week long periods of solitude. "You are a people person, " she said. It is true I value and need human contact. But I have discovered I can also function alone and be content. Somehow this is not a surprise to me. When David became ill I dropped all my outside interests except for graduate school. In the beginning I simply could not face people. I felt shame. I was labile and frightened, but as time passed I discovered I liked being alone. To this day I am not the "people person" I once was. Solitude has emerged as a nurturing friend who has taught me to see and to listen with new understanding.

What other discoveries emerged this week? How has this visit differed from that of winter? Did I glimpse paradise? Perhaps of greatest significance is my recognition that when I am inside Homestead Cabin, physically contained by its log boundaries, I turn inside myself. My inner landscape of contemplation and self analysis emerge. Memories surface. I think about relationships, my womanhood, my life, my work.

Because Spring has urged me into the outer landscape a great portion of this visit, my psyche followed her call. Spring's vital canvas and soundtrack led me outside myself. I focused on her teeming life and labored in her abundance. I immersed myself in her domain. She, not I, usually played the protagonist.

Spring, unlike winter, was a cornucopia of abundance. She spurred active participation in her orgy of life. Lacking winter's profound quiet, spring never offered me the spiritual sanctuary I felt in February. I now understand why churches and cathedrals are quiet places, why "be still and know that I am God" is our instruction for discovering spirituality.

Did I glimpse Paradise or tread the Elysian fields of Greek mythology? Paradise, I have concluded, is heaven. A spiritual place. A mystical realm. No, I did not enter Paradise. Its destination eluded me. But the Greeks' Elysian fields, a place of "song and sunlight," of sweet air and cool breezes, came to me as I lay in the fragrant grasses. My mind was free from want. My body was free from constraints. Unencumbered, I became the grasses and the flowers. I sang with the birds and flew with the honeybees. Sound and sight filled me with their tenderness and vitality. If the Elysian fields are such as this, I knew them of a Sunday afternoon when I let go of my "self."

SUMMER

Interior

It was early afternoon when I blew a farewell kiss to my husband. He watched me pull the cord on the Yamaha and turn the bass boat toward the island. We had just spent a week up here with our daughter, Molly, son, Paul, and his friend Scott. Only David was missing. He was too far away working in California to join us.

It had been a week packed with activity: a week of sailing, canoeing and fishing, of playing hearts, Chinese checkers and chess. A week of repairing gutters, replacing the toilet gasket, and felling a dead birch. A week of feasting on pancakes and sausage, walleye and steak.

Laughter and horseshoes rang in the air. "And it's going to fall in for a single," brought lusty cheers as Kirby Pucket trotted to first base. The chainsaw roared from the woods. Logs splintered under an ax. Lawnmowers rumbled on the mainland. Trolling motors purred near the rushes. Even the natural world offered its voices. Birds chirped. Bees buzzed. Mosquitoes hummed. Thunder filled the heavens and rain pummeled the earth. Through all of this the loons called and laughed on the lake, catching the spirit of the week. And of my family.

As I walked into Homestead Cabin I expected relief and euphoria to rush through me. All the noise and people were finally gone. Quiet and solitude were now mine to savor. Instead, I slumped onto the sofa and stared at the emptiness and silence. The neatness. My throat tightened. I could not contain the tears spilling down my cheeks. Uncannily I yearned for the mess the boy's clothes and games strewn on the floor. Molly's books piled by the easy chair. Cans of Dr. Pepper and Hershey wrappers left on the counter. Tools and fishing lures scattered on the porch. I missed it all. I wanted my family back. My twenty three years of raising children were soon to be history. Paul, my youngest, was leaving for college in three weeks. Only on holidays or vacations would my home shelter the sounds of youth. After Paul's departure, it would feel like this cabin and look like this cabin. Neat and quiet.

I suppose I have been ignoring what my life will look like without any children. After this particularly happy week the picture came into view and I could not bear its image. I plunged into the uncertainty of who I would be and how my life would feel when my identity of being "mom" ended. The solitude this afternoon illuminated a life that seemed lifeless.

I began remembering the joy I felt when I first held Molly. She was so delicate, so beautiful, so perfect. Her coloring and features were her father's. I would later learn her disposition would be his as well. When she was given to me her tiny hand clasped my finger with surprising strength. We bonded at that moment. I remembered the cold chill which ran through me at David's birth, when silence filled the room, and doctors rushed in and surrounded him, and my incredible relief when I heard his faint cry. And I remembered how Paul searched for my breast and kneaded me as he suckled, and then fell peacefully asleep in my arms. I remembered Molly begging for stories and emptying the bookcase and being dismayed that the books had "all writing, no pictures." I remembered David losing his beloved pillowcase the day we moved to Rochester, and crying himself to sleep, and finding it the next spring in the garden, and he did not care anymore. I remembered Paul sucking his thumb as he fearlessly raced his big wheel one handed down the sidewalk. I remembered Molly bringing home a Happy O'Gram saying she had learned to skip. And she skipped all over the house. I remembered David playing Tarzan wearing only a washcloth, and leaping from chair to chair. I remembered Paul saving all his money for baseball cards and hitting his first ball off the T, and seeing the amazement on his face. I remembered Molly wanting to be an actress after playing an angel in her first play. I remembered David and Paul sorrowfully burying our cat, "Mike," and constructing a twig cross to mark his grave. I remembered our family's camping trips where we sat on logs around glowing embers feasting on gooey S'mores and the children asking their father to tell his "Starbuster" story once more. I remembered the children's birthday dinners they got to choose and their excitement over who might get the piece of cake with the quarter I had hidden.

Paul Auster in *The Invention of Solitude* understood my sliding through the past unable to stop, when he wrote: " ... it is only in the darkness of solitude that the work of memory begins." Where will I find such sweet memories in my future? These years are irrefutably over. They will never be again.

It startled me that these memories could leave me so bereft. I was one of those "women of a certain age" eager to embrace the freedom that I had earned. I was that woman ready to soar   the one who had confronted February's bleak silence with joy and expectation. I knew she must still be alive, but this afternoon solitude had a different countenance   one I had not met on my other sojourns. I felt abandoned and lonely. Lost.

I discovered being left alone was far different from leaving to be alone. Perhaps my immersion into solitude's waters was too sudden. I had not had time to take a breath. There were no hours of preparation, no 300 mile drive listening to music and musing about what I might discover at my destination.

It was hours before I moved from the couch. When I arose it was almost supper time. Methodically I made preparations. I ate in the kitchen to avoid the memories still lingering in the porch.

Afterwards I prodded myself to go outside. I knew I must shake this melancholy. A week of solitude awaited me and I wanted to remember it with some measure of satisfaction. I walked down to the lake. The sun was hovering low in the sky as I decided to launch the canoe   its red likeness shimmered hopefully beside me. Heading east I glided through the tall rushes, empathetic with their sighs as the canoe bow parted them. I stayed close to the shore watching schools of tiny green fish swim in and out of the pliant rushes, their bodies spattered with sunlight. Shortly the sandy bottom was covered by feathery water milfoil, suggesting a bonsai forest of conifers. Then blackness, as the lake plunged into an abyss. My attention had been so focused on the lake's underwater forest I had gradually paddled away from shore.

I pointed the canoe toward the familiar channel leading to the south portion of Whitefish Lake. Soon I passed a mass of yellow waterlilies, each bloom the size of a communion cup. Their large heart shaped leaves floated listlessly over long spindly stems. Nearby the white waterlilies had already closed their petals for the night. I studied their perfectly round leaves deeply notched at the base. I felt soothed by the lake's preparation for slumber. When I reached the channel, shadows deepened perceptibly. The sun had now slipped below the treeline. Then something gray caught my attention. I stopped the canoe and backed up as my momentum had carried me by. It was a piece of driftwood so startling in its configuration I first thought it was an antler. I picked it up. On close inspection it looked like a creature whose head was a fish gasping for breath. The body suggested a diver in mid air, bending at the hips before straightening out. A long graceful arm reached toward its feet. I kept the driftwood creature.

As I rounded the western tip of the island heading back, I spotted a beaver swimming toward its lodge. I could only discern his head, but his wake cut a streak so fine and clear, there was no doubt about his identity. The wake created a dynamic action in the inert lake, reminding me of Barnett Newman's sublime color fields also vitalized by bands such as this. I drew closer. Suddenly the beaver dived, slapping his tail flat against the water's surface so loudly I was surprised and dropped a paddle. Quickly I retrieved it. Soon I spotted him again, steering toward his home of chiseled trunks and young saplings.

Beaver are the only mammals other than humans who alter the environment to suit their needs. This ability is apparent along the banks of our lake where there are four lodges, some of which contain trees from our island. Last week we discovered a birch taken down near our cabin. Chiseled markings confirmed the woodsman was a beaver. The next morning we noted the beaver had come back to remove the branches. I was impressed. He remembered where to return with all the miles of shoreline. I suppose that birch now serves as part of his lodge and its tender branches have supplemented his foodstore.

As I paddled toward home the sun's last slanting rays shone on the rushes, turning them to gold for a few exquisite seconds. A gentle wind caressed them. Their reflections merged with their slender forms in the black water. I pulled the canoe up on the bank and flipped it on its side. Slowly I trudged up to the cabin with my piece of driftwood. Now I sit at the kitchen table on which my books and papers are scattered. They comfort me in their possibilities. The driftwood creature hangs on a nail in the living room where I can see it from my chair. It is forever poised to dive deep into unknown waters.

MONDAY JULY 27

The calendar informs me it is just past high summer, but the chill in the air suggests autumn is close at hand. Yet the sweet clover is so profuse it dots the yard like spilled popcorn. The air may be uncertain about the season, but the landscape is not.

As I write this morning, the warmth of the fire is chasing the chill out of the cabin. My sensibilities are calming and my spirits are rising. Perhaps it is the morning light. It seems to have a remarkable capacity to alter one's outlook. I am beginning to understand that yesterday's confrontation with loss illuminated one of solitude's dangers. I succumbed to self pity and depression. I focused on what was over. I lost sight of why I was here which has often sustained me. Alone, without the familiar expectations of family and community, I nose-dived. I became immobilized. When memories surged through me my future seemed bleak and profoundly empty.

But this morning I resolved unhappiness can also be a positive force. Only when we are dissatisfied do we seek understanding and initiate change. It took re entering solitude to force me to confront my feelings about the new stage of life I now enter. I had to acknowledge feelings I had been flippantly denying. I *will* miss my children, even though I have told friends I am eagerly anticipating life without them. I am not as supremely secure as I pretended to believe. As I mused about the sweet memories of yesterday I began to realize why I was given them. They did not flow to remind me of what I would no longer have. They came to me so I *would* remember. I must treasure them as I go forward, and allow them to sustain and nurture me. Today I began to recognize my future does not necessarily prescribe a poorer life. Just a different one. Perhaps even a richer one.

Anthony Storr in his book, *Solitude* writes, "Man's extraordinary success as a species springs from his discontent, which compels him to employ his imagination. ...he possesses an inner world of imagination which is different from, though connected to, the world of external reality." He suggested when we can "bridge" the gap between the two, we find our creative potential. Yesterday I picked up a piece of driftwood. I recognized it was driftwood. Yet my imagination saw it with something more   a fish/person poised to dive into unknown waters. I journeyed beyond external reality, yet never entirely severed the connection. Though I neither solved a problem nor discovered a better way of doing something, my imagination enlightened me. Today I discovered the diver is me, poised to enter an unknown future   the middle years of my life. The driftwood is now a palpable reminder of who I am at this time. My future is uncertain, but I no longer fear it. I am ready to dive and swim in the greater solitude ahead.

While I need human relationships, I also recognize I desire some kind of fulfillment relevant to myself alone. Perhaps this is one aspect of why I am here at the island recording my reflections. No one else can fulfill this need. I have noticed I am not alone in this endeavor. The proliferation of autobiographical work is greater than I ever remember. People like myself, with no particular distinction, are writing their memoirs. My father did. Last week my husband and I met eighty year old Hazel Chumley who lives across the lake. Immediately she told us she was writing her memoirs. It seems we are all attempting to find meaning in our lives. I suppose this is fundamental to being human. We want to understand what shaped us, who affected us, why we have become who we are. We want to feel significant. I have discovered that though relationships are important I need something more. Something which is uniquely mine. Will it be writing? Art? Teaching? Or will I find the ultimate meaning in my life in the spiritual realm? I guess time will reveal the answers. Because human relationships are never without flaws, I think our searches are often solitary ones. Perhaps this is why my father, Hazel, and I chose the solitary experience of writing to make a coherent narrative of our lives.

Late this afternoon the sun grew warm. A northwesterly wind whipped across the lake. I pulled on my swimsuit and zipped up my lifejacket. It was sailing weather! I waded out to the moored Sunfish, raised the sail, secured the halyard and slid in the centerboard. Scrambling into the cockpit, I set a northeasterly course across the wind. No one was in sight. The wind was fairly steady, but intermittently a particularly strong gust darkened the water and filled the sail with surprising force. Instinctively, I turned into the wind to empty the bulging sail, determined not to capsize in the cold water. I have discovered my sailing objectives are the antithesis of my son, Paul's. His greatest joy is to use the wind to capsize. Mine is to join the wind and stay upright. I find capsizing exhausting and threatening. It taxes all my strength to right the boat, and I fear being struck by the boom. Paul is strong and agile. He easily climbs onto the centerboard and the boat rights itself instantly. It occurred to me our different approaches to sailing were similar to our stages in life. Paul's aggressive approach illustrates the young's confidence in their immortality. Mine reflects the reasonable caution we possess by forty nine.

The greatest joy of sailing lies in its capacity to enthrall the senses. Today I felt the sun browning my arms and face, the air combing through my hair, my muscles cleanly contracting when I gripped the mainsheet and guided the tiller. I was prepared for any contingency. My eyes squinted at the sun dazzled water. When the wind filled the sail I trimmed it taut and the boat heeled perfectly. Spray cooled my neck and wet my lips. The wind swooned in my ears. For a fleeting moment I was flying. I had become a bird riding out an updraft. Time and place dissolved in the sun, the spray and the wind. I was immersed in a Homer painting. Then the moment vanished, the wind died, and a deerfly stung my ankle. As I slapped it I released the tiller. About to jibe, I frantically attempted to regain control. In command once more, I began watching the shimmering water for the next shadow signifying another possibility of euphoria. Of earthly paradise.

Today dawned clear and cold. After a breakfast of orange juice, toast, and a soft boiled egg, I slipped on my buffalo plaid flannel shirt and took to the woods. Last week I was anxious to explore them, but discovered the midsummer brush and tangled thickets were too dense to negotiate. Vines entwined my ankles. Branches scratched my arms and face. Dissatisfied with only the path between Homestead Cabin and Birchwood, I hauled the ancient Sears mower out of the toolshed and entered the woods. The mower and I were invincible. Through brush and grasses, mosses and ferns, saplings and bushes, over fallen trees and decaying stumps we persevered. I had no map. No guideposts. The former deer trails had vanished after the deer departed before spring's thaw. I simply went where the mower and I could go. My goal was to create trails, from one end of the island to the other. If I felt like creating a fork or "Y," I did. Sometimes I mowed great circles to surprise the hiker. I worked from three locations on the island. Poplar Cabin, Birchwood Cabin, and The Bunkhouse. My greatest difficulty was connecting the trails. I did not want to create a maze with no destination. By day's end I had clear cut and connected passages throughout the length of the island and much of its breadth.

Two summers ago was the only other time I mowed trails. The following spring I remembered how exciting it was to walk where I had never been. I also made a marvelous discovery. On the western end of the island grew hundreds of Yellow Lady's Slippers. There is a deep satisfaction in entering the woods alone and discovering its secrets. My family thinks that I am "eccentric" for mowing paths for hours. I suppose I am. But my solitary labor has changed my relationship to the island. By altering its landscape like the beaver, I too have been nourished. My trails are like his gnawed birch stumps   markers signifying my interaction with the natural world. I thrive here as well.

And so this morning I followed the trails I made last week. I came upon a white pine so magnificent it was spared by loggers years ago. The woods about me were lush with their mature foliage. The cool wet summer had nourished such ferns as Maidenhair and Brackon and carpets of mosses in apple, grass, and forest greens. Mushrooms with caps of ochre, red, and brown dotted the forest floor. Golden cabbage like fungi perched atop stumps and fallen trees. In all directions were the broken, leaning trees I had observed on earlier visits. The green coffin around them did not soften their still grotesque silhouettes. But nearby I was heartened to see saplings reaching for light. A new generation of life had been spawned.

What was absent in the woods were wildflowers. I saw none. The only summer flowers were in the island's open spaces   the elegant Showy Lady's Slippers, Oxeye Daisies, and Blackeyed Susans at Birchwood, and the Sweet Clover at the Homestead. I knew many other species grew up here. While driving in to the mainland dock last week, I counted no less than seven; however such flowers as the Cow Parsnip, Purple Loosestrife, Common Yarrow, and Indian Paintbrush did not make it across the lake's expanse. Later I read in *Northland Wild Flowers* that many wildflowers are "fussy" about soil chemistry, particularly its alkalinity or acidity. Also, each requires precise amounts of soil moisture and shade. Since I saw these wildflowers along the road, I suspect our wooded landscape does not provide the necessary habitat for them to thrive.

Throughout my walk I attempted to tread noiselessly, hoping some creature might appear. I did not succeed. Twice I spotted droppings, but I did not know to whom they belonged. Eventually I sat down in a grassy area, thinking this might elicit a rabbit or even a raccoon. In the past we have observed both, as well as woodchucks, squirrels, porcupines, and fox. But no creature appeared. I leaned against a dead elm. The lush tree canopies dappled the earth in kinetic patterns of light and shadow. The landscape was a luxuriant green and I thought of the Greeks' Elysian fields. In the distance a bird I could not identify was singing. While listening to his music I imagined he was Pan playing his pipes, serenading his lovely domain. I tried to memorize his sweet refrain but lost it soon after the notes ceased. Later I arose and made my way back without a wrong turn.

Tonight I walked down to our deck, perched above the lake. The sun had long set, but its afterglow remained of pale pinks and deep blues. Against this pastel canvas were the black silhouettes of white pines, maples, and birches. The lake was so glassy the trees' reflections merged into their forms. In the northwestern sky I noticed a dark thundercloud looming. I wondered if a storm was coming.

Now I sit here in the kitchen. Drawings lie on the floor, by the toaster, and on this table. I have been sketching visions that willow or driftwood could make palpable. Among them are "Solitude" comprised of a single bough rising from whiteness, a "Destination" piece where a dock enters an unseen vista, "Wind / Reflection" where angled slender forms are suspended in the obscure boundaries of reality and reflection. For this, I do not know what materials I will use. I also sketched some twig pieces which might pay homage to Pan and a wall piece of dark willow boughs paying homage to Franz Kline. Why these images presented themselves I can only surmise. Their arrival may seem to have been effortless, but since February I have been contemplating the events and images from my sojourns here, yearning to discover some visual responses I could create. This afternoon while dozing by the woodstove, these particular images surfaced. I arose and began sketching. Though these visions may change in my constructions, I am grateful I can return to them as I first imagined them.

WEDNESDAY JULY 29

In that mysterious place between sleep and consciousness I saw myself rooted here on this island   connected like the limb to the tree. I am beginning to understand how a place can transform you, make you into its own likeness. Its rhythms have become my rhythms. I awaken to its light. Thrive in its warmth. Retreat in its cold. Its isolation is my isolation. Its frenzy my frenzy. Its solitude my solitude. Gretel Ehrlich also observed this connection between the land and its inhabitants in *The Solace of Open Spaces*. In her preface, she wrote, "I had suffered a tragedy... What I *had* lost... was my appetite for life. ...I went to Wyoming. Friends asked when I was going to stop 'hiding out'... What appeared to them as a landscape of lunar desolation... was luxurious to me. For the first time I was able to take up residence on earth... "

I have also discovered this island is my teacher. I am its student in a one room schoolhouse. I have learned to discern time by the heavenly bodies and read fronts in the wind. Deer inform me where to walk. The swallow how to nurture. I have learned when voices travel across the lake the humidity is high. When the ground under my feet trembles, I am on a bog. Logs split cleanly when it is cold. Birch bark is better kindling than newspaper. Yellow bellied sapsuckers are artists. When Orion is visible in the sky it is winter.

I have observed this island confronts life directly and simply, informing me again that there is a season to be born and a season to die. I have learned to be Thoreau's "self appointed inspector of snow, storms and rain storms... " Thoreau also was a student when he went to Walden. "I went to the woods because I wished to live deliberately, to front only the essential facts of life, and see if I could not learn what it had to teach... " I think we both believed the natural world had lessons for us to learn, but we differed in our goals. Thoreau was seeking *how* to live, whereas I have been seeking where life's perfection lies. Is it in the exterior world? Or does it lie in our interior one?

There was also another teacher with me today   my son David. He called me from California. Quietly and with surprising conviction he said, "Mom, my life now belongs to God. This is how I will live." His insight into understanding faith as more than an intellectual exercise reminded me of Thomas Merton, who wrote in *Thoughts in Solitude*, "The spiritual life is first of all a *life*. It is not merely something to be known and studied, it is to be lived." In all honesty I was startled by David's new found faith, for only a few years ago he was a confirmed atheist. His youthful spirituality died when drugs and illness enveloped him. Suddenly, he has found a faith which seems to reach to the core of his being. His convictions were so encompassing I sensed a need to take inventory of my own faith   one I knew to be primarily cerebral. I felt like a student as I listened to my son explain his beliefs and describe their impact on his life.

However, I am uneasy. I cannot deny David is vulnerable. Perhaps his spiritual awakening has arisen out of loneliness in California and living with Christians whose faith is passionate and persuasive. I want to believe that David's conversion experience has depth and substance. Clearly he has changed. Whether his new spirituality is one of substance or a euphoria explained by his illness, time will reveal. Whatever transpires, I hope it will be a prelude to an ongoing spiritual awareness. Spirituality, I believe, will be instrumental in his recovery. Of this I am certain. The faith of both Merton and David has stirred me to examine my own. They have reminded me that the spiritual life is not abstract, but a tangible life to be lived.

THURSDAY JULY 30

For the first time in these sojourns to the island, I awakened at dawn. Out the window sanguine pinks shimmered on the horizon, promising a lovely day. Mist rose in swells from the lake, secreting the distant shore. To the west the world was lost in a sweep of impenetrable gray. Eagerly I left my warm sleeping bag, picked up my camera and headed to our deck perched above the lake. In all my years I have only witnessed a handful of sunrises. I have always been what people call an "owl." I thrive at night and find my nourishment under the cover of darkness. Early morning usually finds me unfit company. This morning I envied the "larks" who have memories of sunrises such as that today.

The lake was silent as I contemplated the dawn of another day. Motionless, I listened to the soundlessness of solitude. Then I focused my camera and snapped a picture. The click of the shutter was an unexpected intrusion. Its sound startled a solitary loon poised in the center of the lake, and he called out to me. I set the camera down. Was the point of my awakening to capture this vista on film? It was unquestionably my first impulse. But I should have known a photograph could not record this sublime morning. Its edges would edit what I had observed. Its flat surface could not encompass the immense silence surrounding me, or that mournful refrain of the loon's voice. I turned my gaze to the east. As the invisible sun illuminated the sky, the low lying mist began to dissipate. Soon trees came into focus. Docks emerged. It was as if I were looking at a Polaroid snapshot slowly revealing recognizable images. Then the magic was over. The familiar world I knew was again in place. I walked back to Homestead Cabin and blissfully slipped into my sleeping bag.

After a light breakfast I went outside. It suddenly struck me I heard no beating of wings as I opened the porch door. When the family arrived last week, we spotted three gray fuzzballs cradled in the nest under the eave. Early this week I noted the babies were now perched on top of the nest, not in it. Each sported a beak outlined in yellow and tiny dark eyes which peered fixedly at me. Throughout this time the mother swallow made countless trips to and from her nest bringing insects to her young. Her diligence has now been rewarded. The nest is empty. Her children are flying.

My musings soon turned to my three children and my dream of the day they too will fly. Independent, competent, and self assured. Is not this the goal of all creatures on this planet? I have accepted that my children need more time than others to "fly" unassisted, but I am perceiving some growth.

David's spiritual odyssey is ongoing. In part his journey seems to be a search for understanding why he has suffered the ordeal of his psychosis. More important, I think he is discovering a spiritual foundation which permits him to see a future that offers purpose and meaning. Perhaps I am choosing to see what I know is vital to his recovery, but I am permitting myself a measure of hopefulness. His voice and new found faith seem strong and convincing.

My eldest, Molly, is my passionate child, and possesses the fervent drive I occasionally glimpse in myself. She lives life with the greatest intensity of my children, which has led her to know not only life's summits but also its valleys   plummeting her into abysses of despair. Since childhood Molly's particular passion has been theater. She left home at thirteen to attend the Children's Theatre School in Minneapolis   then went on to Barnard College, where she slipped into inertia and insecurity. Now she is struggling to complete her theatre arts degree. In a long conversation last week, I witnessed a profound change in her. For the first time she was accepting personal responsibility for her past. She has sought help and is reaching deep within herself to discover the necessity of honest reflection. Now Molly speaks of goals and understands only she can realize them. A new self assurance radiated from her voice and eyes. My spirits soared. It occurred to me that for the first time she and I were riding the same wave. We were both struggling to reach the shore without toppling. We both had goals we needed to realize, and instinctively knew we could not divert our eyes. We both sought diplomas filled in with our names.

My youngest child, Paul, seems to live life with the greatest ease of my three children, adapting to its buffeting nature. His natural optimism finds the positive in this world. He reminds me of the hidden city Raisa, which Italo Calvino described in *Invisible Cities*. In this city of sadness, a fleeting moment of joy could be found at every moment. Paul departs for college soon and though I know he will confront hurdles, I am confident he will surmount them. Perhaps one's youngest child profits from his place in the family.

As I sit here daring to imagine my children flying like the young swallows, I am aware once again that my nest will soon be empty. The hours after my family departed informed me I too have a life to create and preparations to make. From my solitary musings here, I have discovered marriage has not filled the void, nor even would my children's "flying like the swallows." I wondered if working, full-time, would be the source of fulfillment.

I live in a society where more women work outside the home than in it. Thirty years ago I happily chose marriage and family as my vocation. This was what I knew and I fulfilled the legacy of my small town upbringing. Betty Friedan's *The Feminine Mystique* was published the year I was married   too late to alert me to other possibilities, too late for me to observe that I was a product of a society whose ideal woman stayed at home to raise a family. However, I was aware of one woman who was creative   our next door neighbor who was an artist and a writer and sent her stories to *The New Yorker* and *The Atlantic Monthly*. Though she was not published, she took great pride in at least having rejection slips from magazines she highly regarded. I have never ceased to respect her high standards or forgotten her deep satisfaction in pursuing something which was uniquely hers.

Paradoxically, women today have the opposite dilemma. Because of our economy, many women find they *must* work. They do not have the option of choosing to stay home and raise their children. I suppose the ideal society is one where either choice is respected and possible.

However, my particular dilemma lies within myself, not society. What will I do now? What do I want to do? How will I contribute to my family and society and fill the void which awaits me? Though my family's economic circumstances do not require my working, I know any income I could generate would ease the burden of college expenses.

The graduate work I am pursuing lies in the arts. Unquestionably this is where my interests, talents, and education point in my future decisions. But in what context? Like my neighbor, I will create. I yearn to find if I can write or visually create work I value enough to publish and send to juried exhibitions. I think by middle age we have lived long enough to have something to say. We have endured. We have discovered how to edit what is irrelevant. Hopefully we are becoming free from others' expectations and the "shoulds" which burden us in our early years. This is the time we can tell our stories, reveal the truths we have learned, take risks.

As I consider my past art, much of it was a response to others' expectations. It did not give voice to a personal vision. Now it seems important to create work which speaks to what is essential. These goals of mine do not guarantee income, however. Contributing economically to my family is the other path which beckons me. Yet simply making money is an anathema.

As I sit here musing about my future, I can hear the evening chorus outside the cabin. Each creature is singing its song. Each creature knows its work. How good it would be to possess such certain knowledge. I suppose the option I see most clearly is teaching. This would not only be intellectually satisfying, but also I would be making a contribution I consider valuable.

It has occurred to me that these are the same concerns my children voice. "What should I do, who am I?" they ask. My pat answer is always the same. "You are what you value and do." It seems we will know what our work or vocation is when we cease asking and are finally doing. Perhaps I simply need a measure of patience.

Not until this journal I am writing have I confronted these issues. This solitary journey has revealed more than I bargained for or expected. Never had I questioned my past art. Never had I been critical of my work in terms of its personal vision. Never had I seriously considered my future. The solitude here has revealed who I am and who I might become. Its silence has been a profound vehicle for confrontation. You cannot hide from who you are as you face the naked realities that define your existence.

I broke my solitude today. Before my husband left for home, he took the living room window to Blackduck for repair, and asked me to pick it up. I promised I would. The cabin could not be left open to the elements. Meanwhile Hazel Chumley called. She is our new acquaintance across the lake. Hazel had noticed my light. Last week my husband and I invited her to a play in Bemidji. At eighty, she no longer drives into town   only to her mailbox at the end of her two mile driveway. Hers is the driveway Byron Bromley pointed out on my venture to Blackduck last spring. Hazel lives alone on the lake six months of the year, and was "delighted" to meet neighbors so close by. Her call was an invitation to visit. I could not turn her down. We agreed I would come today.

Hazel is also the lady writing her memoir, and reminds me of Ruben's women and the women my father likes. She is not slight, but full and round. This afternoon she was wearing a white turtleneck under a denim jumper which fell easily over her generous body. Her bright eyes seemed bluer than the night we took her to the theater, but her easy laughter was the same. It completes many of her sentences and I always sense she finds life joyful and carefree. Her short white hair is as casual as her laughter. Her lips are full and sensual. She is not pretty. Her features are too large. Yet her face radiates beauty in its expressiveness. She always looks directly into my eyes when she is speaking. I cannot dismiss her presence.

When I arrived at her door after my trip to Blackduck, Hazel eagerly ushered me to an easy chair. Beside me was a stack of papers, pamphlets, and books. She pulled out a slender volume of women's writings published by the Women's Resource Center of Bemidji State University. Included was an excerpt from her memoir. Then she handed me a bound copy of the speeches she and her husband, "Chum," once delivered on aging at Rochester Methodist Hospital. Deeper in the pile were numerous reprints of research she had done at

77

Sloan Kettering, and wildlife essays published in the Minneapolis Tribune. I was duly impressed by her prodigious array of accomplishments.

But it was the memoir that she handed me last. I soon noted two beginnings labeled "A" and "B." Hazel asked me to read them and tell her which was better. She could not decide. As I began to read, she went into the kitchen to make us cranberry grapefruit coolers. Soon she appeared with two frosty glasses and a plate of Oreo cookies and slices of her zucchini bread. I felt her eyes on me as I read and sipped and ate. Glancing up once, I noticed her face eager and expectant. I continued reading somewhat anxiously. I sensed my sought after opinion would determine those first pages of her memoir. The final triumphant work of her life. Fortunately my task was easier than I expected after reading through version "B."

Both texts described her tragic birth in Minneapolis 1913, when her mother died of septicemia from lack of sanitary procedures. In version "A," Hazel wrote in the first person from her grandmother's point of view. It was an astute choice, as she had learned her birth story from her grandmother. The language was simple and captured not only the drama of the event but also the personality of her grandmother.

The "B" version reflected Hazel's disciplined years of research, editing manuscripts, and writing abstracts. This style was a list of the events in chronological order. It succinctly recorded background information on her parents and defined purpura fever. Though fine writing for a journal article, it lacked the power I felt in version "A."

Hazel beamed with gratitude. Over the next two hours I sat listening to her tell her story. Her sharp memory took me to a boarding house on Hennepin Street in Minneapolis where she was raised by her grandmother who died when Hazel was thirteen. Her father who had remarried did not want her, so she went to work as a nanny, and eventually put herself through high school and the University of Minnesota.

Hazel's story mesmerized me. In those two hours I do not recall speaking except to respond now and then when appropriate. I left her sitting on a gold velveteen easy chair surrounded by her books and papers, and her adopted daughter's landscape paintings. Begun in childhood, the paintings lined the entire length of the room. They mirrored the lake and woods out the window behind Hazel. But it was her daughter's self portrait, hanging in the hallway on which I lingered.

It was reminiscent of Rouault's richly colored faces outlined in bold black strokes. A lovely confident woman gazed at me. I knew why.

I drove back to the landing feeling a little guilty that I had broken my solitude, for I had come up here with the idea I would see no one. My solitude would be pure. I had not wanted to call Byron during my winter pilgrimage, or use his assistance in spring, but both had been necessary. I suppose tonight I felt I had compromised my resolve once more. By the time I reached the island I accepted the possibility I might do so again in autumn. Hazel's significance to me can be seen in my writing tonight. Her vitality and humor were unquestionably appealing. But how she lives her life is a parable on how to live in this world. What I understood as I boated home at dusk was why she is so "rich." Her solitude overflowed with memories. She allowed them to nurture her and sustain her, just as I discovered mine must when I was mourning the loss of my children the day I arrived. Hazel's entry into my solitude can only be construed as a gift to be gracefully accepted.

SATURDAY AUGUST 1

It is because my wounded psyche is healing that I am not ready to depart. Solitude's undemanding nature has been a soothing tonic, clarifying the jumble of painful feelings I felt on my arrival. She is a sweet elixir an antidote to counteract depression. I have been swept up by her healing powers. Though my psyche may relapse tomorrow, I have learned separating oneself from the expectations of this world is imperative. It has been so for me. I realize in Rochester I frequently present the "face" to the world it expects to see. When acquaintances ask how I am, I answer "fine" when I am not, because people do not really want to hear my problems. When the psychiatrist advises me to be patient with David, I assure him I am, when I know I have faltered and will do so again. I pretend I am happy for other families' children who are having success when I cannot bear the comparison.

Only *I* know the player I have become in this script I inhabit. My solitude at this island has been necessary for me to discover life's sweetness again. It has been like an injection of penicillin. The pain of discovering who I am wanes when I lie in the sun's healing warmth. Here I am permitted to do nothing. Say nothing. Be nothing. This landscape relieves me of expectations. It gently reawakens my senses. I notice the songs of the birds, the heightened fragrance of the woods in the coolness of night. In solitude and stillness I hear the lake softly lapping the shore. I look at the sky and rediscover the beauty of blue. The world has become good again. Yes, it has been imperative for me to separate myself from the world's expectations. Now this incontrovertible fact must find a format when I return home. My need for physical solitude will have to adapt to the limitations of living with others. But at least I am confronting myself, my children, and my life with open eyes. None of us are perfect. I must remember this. I suppose my notion of "paradise" appears to be an illusion now, but deep within, I still refuse to believe it does not exist. I shall continue to search. Somewhere it lies waiting patiently, expectantly.

In this island setting it seems close at hand. The warmth of the sun today filled the landscape with dance. Nature asked nothing more than to exist. Its character was empowering as it once again led me to the world of my senses. My anxieties ceased to exist for a while. The ongoing rhythms reflected some grand mysterious force at work.

Hazel called me today to say good bye. I was glad. Our friendship was immediate and rich and good. She promised to write when the fall color was peaking. "Bye, Dear, I really will miss you," were her parting words. I felt likewise. This island sojourn has not ended in solitude but in companionship. I appreciate that both are indispensable to human fulfillment.

AUTUMN

Emergence

SATURDAY, OCTOBER 10

I received a postcard from Hazel last month. As I drove north to the island, I was envious of the autumn beauty she described. I knew I would be fortunate if even a remnant of her description remained. "Trees are blazing in red and orange," she wrote, "framing the lake like an old fashioned gilt mirror, with clouds and sky reflected in it." Now, four weeks later, I hoped to see autumn's second show   the golden one.

When I reached the lakes south of ours I saw them. In the late afternoon light the tamarack pines shone with a gold more golden than any maple could imagine. The sun lent their feathery needles a surreal countenance. I pulled over to etch into my memory a landscape of blue sky, deep green firs, and pale pillars of aspen and birch   each enhanced by the luminous gold tamaracks.

A cool northwesterly wind hailed my arrival at Whitefish Lake, but color was spare. The aspen and birch gingerly held on to a smattering of yellow leaves. Only a solitary tamarack welcomed me across the lake. The stark silhouettes of winter had already taken possession of the landscape.

I stacked my gear on the dock. Nearby was the bass boat, supported on a series of logs leading down to the water. The logs and gravity made the launching simple. After attaching the motor I loaded my goods   duffle, food bag, cooler, and a box of books and papers. Then I returned for the gas can which each owner stores under the aluminum boat. It was light. Too light. Unscrewing the cap I estimated perhaps a half cup of fuel remained. After six hours on the road, I refused to drive to Blackduck. I could not muster the will or energy to get back into my car. Hoping the motor had not been totally emptied, I decided to take a chance. I also counted on finding gas stored in the tool shed.

85

The motor started on the first pull. Elated, I headed toward the right of the small island before ours. This would place me closest to our island's shoreline. Normally we go to the other side where the passage is wider. The motor sputtered and died thirty yards from the small island. I cursed the former visitor for committing this oversight. Only one paddle was in the boat. I slowly made my way to the shallow passage. Once there I poled my way through the rushes. Reaching the open lake again, I discovered the wind was blowing directly at our island. Gratefully I let it assist me. Finally I was near our shoreline where I poled the boat home. Because of the wind, the entire crossing took me less than forty five minutes. My risk paid off even more grandly when I found a gas can filled to the brim. I did not dwell on the predicament I would have faced had the can been empty.

Weary from my exertions, I rested a moment on the porch swing, but the brisk air prodded me to gather kindling and wood. On the way up here, I heard the temperature was to dip into the twenties. I set a blazing fire in the old Reeve's woodstove and unpacked my clothes, books, and cooler. The mustiness in the cabin rapidly dissipated, replaced by warmth and the sweet hint of woodsmoke. Euphoric with these simple pleasures, I began my dinner preparations. When my pasta was ready I poured a glass of wine and dined at the kitchen table in utter contentment... until some flies joined me. I thought I heard more buzzing emanating from the living room. I went in to look. In the rafters were hundreds of flies aroused by the unexpected warmth. Quickly I searched for a can of Raid. Finding one on the door ledge in the porch, I climbed on a chair and began spraying toward the cabin's roof peak. I emptied the entire can. The intense fumes set me coughing and I knew I had better get outside. Grabbing my jacket and flashlight, I walked out into the night. The clean cold air soothed my lungs and spirit. I headed toward Birchwood Cabin, listening to my footsteps crunching on the fallen leaves. Any creature nearby had ample warning of my presence. The woods were quiet and I envied their ignorance of the nightmare back at the cabin. Reluctantly I turned around after walking as far as the bunkhouse beyond Birchwood cabin.

As I stepped into the living room a dying fly brushed my head on its final descent. Disgusted, I tousled my hair to dispel any more. Hundreds of flies were scattered on the floor, the furniture, the mantle, the beds... many still alive. Their buzzing intensified as they danced tiny circles in their final seconds of life. With the fly swatter I methodically terminated one at a time. Above me a remnant still swarmed but I trusted the Raid had entered their systems. Though the cabin was not as noxious, I cracked a window. I swept the flies into a pile before discarding them in the woodstove. A quick count revealed over 500. Then I vacuumed their remaining fragments. This ordeal lasted an hour. Their death dance still haunts me now as I write. I worry there are more to come and I have no more Raid – only cans of Deep Woods Off. I was prepared for this infestation, but now I am fully aware I am vulnerable should the flies return. This is a feeling I cannot bear. Perhaps one reason I came here was to prove to myself I can handle difficult situations. I will not leave. That I know. If the flies return I will find a solution even if it means driving to Blackduck for more Raid.

I am physically and emotionally spent. This island has a propensity to test one's endurance. Despite knowing this, I still come here anticipating peace and solitude, but each visit has presented trials to overcome. There is that about life we do not control. I have rediscovered I cannot escape adversity even on this lovely island. Instead I must confront what lies at my feet, appalling as it might be. Generally when problems have arisen up here, I have turned to my husband. But these sojourns have forced me to find the solutions. It heartens me that neither being stranded on the lake without gas nor facing the fly infestation frightened me. Instead I felt anger and dismay. I knew what I had to do and did it. Somehow we cope when we must. I have discovered I really can handle the traditionally "masculine" tasks I always said I could, the tasks my sons and Tony would claim as theirs. This island is a remarkable setting for testing one's capacity to cope with the unexpected. It is a training center, a boot camp, a school in basic survival, regardless of gender or age.

SUNDAY OCTOBER 11

My mother was born 77 years ago today. On a frosty morning such as today's, I imagine her in the kitchen preparing Wheatina for my father like she did for me years ago. I cannot recall a morning without breakfast aromas filling the house. "Breakfast is the important meal," she would tell us children. And we always ate, for if we did not, we were clearly "sick" and put to bed. Now I smile at her fervor. One does perform better with morning nourishment. Heeding her motherly advice, I scrambled an egg this morning, promising myself to call her when I return home.

After eating I called Byron Bromley to let him know I had arrived. My husband had asked that I check in with Byron since cold temperatures might freeze the pipes. Byron, too, was anxious and urged me to wrap the pipe leading into the pump house and those inside it. Now two bright orange sleeping bags have found new purposes.

Yesterday's havoc with the flies postponed my unpacking the bag of non perishables. As I put away canned goods, Jif, cereal, crackers, and seasonings, I was amused at the duplication of foods on the shelves. Since we are one third owners of this island, three families use this cabin, and a clear absence of communication is evident. I counted numerous containers of basil, oregano, chili powder, and cumin. A few were empty, others thoroughly cemented. Some probably dated back to our purchase of this place ten years ago. I also discovered we had pasta of every description, three bottles of soy sauce, and more tomato soup than anyone cared to eat. The cabinet suggested a museum display recording the eating habits and penchants of our families. It seems we rarely clean out the cabinet and favor Italian, Chinese, and Mexican cuisine!

The interior of this cabin also reflects a little of the character of us all: what we value, what we enjoy, what we cherish. Driftwood sculptures including the piece I found last spring hang on the wall and rest on the mantle. They have primarily been gathered by the Wilson children and mine. Also displayed are torn, yellowed maps of Whitefish Lake and a brittle (and garish) Paul Bunyan Vacationland map. Paul Bunyan is the lumberjack hero of "tall tales" told in these parts. It is said his footprints created the lakes. Each map is upheld by curling strips of masking tape. A frayed Wordsworth poem hangs beside them, copied in adolescent writing on yellowed paper.

" Oh then the calm
And dead still water lay upon my mind.
Even with a weight of pleasure and the sky.
Never before so beautiful, sank down
Into my heart, and held me like a dream."

A Far Side cartoon of two cowboys about to draw abuts it I suspect my son Paul clipped it and taped it there. He loves Gary Larson's cartoons. This one was cut out of a newspaper.

"OK, when I say 'Draw,' we draw... Ready?
One, two, three Straw!... OK, just checkin your ears...
One, two three Claw! ...OK,
DRAWbridge!... " (Larson).

Etchings of fishing lures, two island photographs and a watercolor landscape by my daughter's boyfriend, Jason, complete the eclectic display.

Also revealing are the magazines and books we have accrued through the years. "In Fisherman," "Bass Pro Shops" and "Field and Stream," are stacked with "Elle," "Art in America," "The Economist," "Minnesota Monthly," and "The New Yorker." Though some of the magazines date back six years, no one pitches them. Who knows that I may wish to re read "Dvorak in Iowa" describing Patricia Hampl's and Steven Sorman's collaboration of *Spillville* in a 1987 copy of "Minnesota Monthly"?

Our books line the length of the mantle. Some date back before we arrived. Like the magazines they speak to our myriad interests. They range from *Barbie Solves a Mystery, Outdoor Safety and Survival,* and *Old Yeller,* to *War and Peace, Art as Experience,* and *The Best American Short Stories of the Eighties.* There is a quip I recall which says you can tell what people are like from their garbage. I suspect what we have *not* thrown out describes us just as accurately.

As I look around this cabin memories surge. I see our history. The children's growing up. My growing older. It amazes me how these simple possessions have become prized relics. I even treasure the outgrown boots and life jackets, the puzzles with missing pieces. For some reason I have never really considered these possessions as important before tonight. I suppose when I am here with my family, I am directed toward people, not place. Today there were no faces or voices to distract me.

Solitude opened my eyes.

There are twelve people who call this island their own, but it is our family who have served as the island's caretakers. The others did not want the responsibility, and were grateful we were willing to open and close the place, do the repairs, maintain the motors, and chop the wood. Despite the labor we have been content with this arrangement. Having spent far more time here, we have gained an intimacy with the island's fabric and its character. We have discovered that we and the landscape nurture one another. Fallen branches and dying trees have provided us with necessary warmth. By removing them, we have provided an open space for sunlight to reach existing trees or foster the birth of a young seedling.

Our relationships with one another have also been affected by our relationship to the land. Up here at the island all our labors have been necessary to survive. This lesson in communal effort has carried over to how we have lived and worked together. Such tasks as preparing meals or cutting and stacking wood have found us all sharing in the labor. But possibly the greatest difference in our behavior here compared to that in Rochester is the restoration of conversation. There it seems the television and radio are too often the voices we hear. Or we physically separate Tony to the bedroom to read, and the children to their rooms with friends. I often find myself alone in the kitchen or go out to my studio. Only at dinner do we gather to talk.

An island, unlike any other piece of land, envelopes its inhabitants in its smells, secret places, and solitary musings because it is self contained. We only leave it for necessities. When we come here, we stay. It has led each of us to self discovery and in some ways has sculpted who we are. It has led my daughter to introspection and to write poetry my husband to master the chainsaw. My son, Paul, has chosen natural resources as his vocation. I think the countless hours he has spent fishing and exploring the island habitat led him to this decision. It led me to desire to explore its solitude and landscape. But more significantly, this island has led me to creativity and a re thinking of what I value. My wooden structure would not exist if I had not come here, nor would I consider the word "ownership" as I do now. No longer do I desire "things" as I once did. Trappings, I have discovered, are essentially inconsequential and impermanent. It is our relationships to one another which endure.

MONDAY OCTOBER 12

Autumn is playing a fugue as she awaits winter's arrival. Each day her cold and wind have played the theme of her certain departure. Today I had to continually stoke the woodstove. Yet the brilliant sun and deep blue lake spoke of warmer, gentler times. They seemed anachronistic as I carried in log after log.

While frying bacon this morning, I gazed out the kitchen window. Nestled in the leaves near the tool shed was a remarkable sight I had not noticed. A toilet bowl was glistening in the sun. The startling white porcelain was juxtaposed with the drab browns and rusts of the leaves. The piece was not only aesthetically pleasing but also spoke to an artwork by the great Dada artist Marcel Duchamp. I suspected Byron Bromley placed the toilet there, as I recalled my husband mentioning Byron was planning to replace the broken one in Poplar Cabin. Now my "Fountain II" exists along with its predecessor, Duchamp's urinal dubbed "Fountain." Duchamp submitted "Fountain" to the Society of Independent Artists in 1917 as a protest against the attitude that art should be considered sacred. His innovative ready-mades led to valuing the intellect and concepts of the artist as well as skill or talent. His impact has been profound and has influenced such important genres as the conceptual art we see today.

I photographed "Fountain II" this afternoon. When I leave I shall take it with me.

Afterwards, I replenished my wood supply, then walked the paths I cleared last spring. Now covered by leaves, they almost merged into the forest floor. I had difficulty determining their boundaries and made some wrong turns; but eventually I traversed the length of the island. Not a bird or creature joined me. Too windy I suppose. The woods are clear cut again exposing sky in every direction. Once more I sensed the island's island character, and felt cradled and secure in its boundaries. The crisp leaves under my feet, the white capped lake, and the smoke scented air were simple and good. Alone, one's capacity to absorb nature's sights, sounds, and smells is heightened because it is what surrounds and confronts you. There is no distracting conversation. Nature rivets your senses. Though I see and feel winter quickly approaching, I am not downcast. In fact, the opposite is true. I love winter. Its emptiness, its cold, its stark landscape inexplicably invigorate me like no other season. It is the season I feel most alive, the season that lifts me out of my ordinary existence.

But I do miss the loons. Ever since I arrived I have strained to hear their plaintive voices. Now I am certain they have departed for warmer waters. Yesterday I was most curious and delighted to see a robin feeding beside the cabin. Surprised, I reached for my bird book. This robin was unquestionably in the wrong place for this time of year according to Roger Tory Peterson. But then perhaps, I am as well, according to some people I know.

The robin was the first bird I recognized as a child. I can remember a bird coloring book which depicted a robin perched on her nest. I colored her breast bright red, even though I knew a "real" robin's breast was rusty brown. Her name "Robin Redbreast" enchanted me and so I chose to mimic her name. Besides, red was far more beautiful than rust or brown.

We tend to think of robins as common and ordinary birds. Yet according to Paul Gruchow in *The Necessity of Empty Places,* robins were once endangered. Uncannily, James Audubon participated in their demise by declaring them "fat and juicy." The toll on them was profound. Later, pesticides contributed to their continued decline. But in 1913 the U.S. Migratory Bird Act was passed protecting them, as well as some other songbirds. Fortunately today robins are once again abundant.

What I found valuable in this account was man's recognizing the importance of the natural world and its inhabitants. I think none of us can conceive the loss we would experience without song birds. In some inexplicable way their clear fresh voices articulate life's essence and promise its fleeting moments of sanity, moments unencumbered by the irrationalities of mankind.

TUESDAY OCTOBER 13

The wind has finally quieted, but the temperature continues to drop. Long underwear has become a necessity along with a continual fire for me to be comfortable. Byron noticed the cold too and called this morning. He asked if I had wrapped the pipes at Poplar Cabin. I had not. He also suggested I check the new toilet for ice, and to flush it if it was not frozen solid. I found some expendable towels and another sleeping bag and dutifully followed his instructions. I was greatly relieved no ice had formed, as Byron had commented if I found any, we would have to "winterize" today. That would mean I would be without water for washing dishes and bathing. "If you keep them pipes covered and flush every morning, you should be okay," Byron advised me one last time before we hung up. I began not only flushing the toilets every few hours but also opening up every spigot. Flowing water became an obsession with me when I contemplated the consequences of it freezing. I am not finding Byron's continuing interest in my welfare intrusive, but a welcome concern of a fellow human being.

I settled down to write when the phone rang again. It was Hazel Chumley. My solitude seems to be in greater jeopardy with each visit here. But I guess I am to blame. I am the one who originally instigated a call to Hazel during our family vacation. In all honesty, I was happy to hear her warm buoyant voice. We chatted about the weather, the short autumn blaze of color, and a shrew which waits by her door to sneak in. I laughed. She mentioned she would be leaving this weekend for New York City where she will spend the winter with her daughter.

I told her I had been taking long walks in the woods. She recommended I wear a hard hat and be prepared to encounter a bear. "Trees fall all the time," she warned, "and just this week I saw a bear when I drove to my mailbox." She told me never to run, and to carry a tin pie plate and a spoon. She had the theory that the noise of beating a tin plate hurts bears' ears and they would scurry away. I smiled to myself. It was good to hear Hazel's charming tales and motherly

95

counsel again. Before hanging up she asked if I would come by Friday. In some way, I am comforted by Hazel's presence across the lake. Is she a parental figure for me? Could I still be desiring the presence of a parent, or am I reminded of my mother's concern and tenderness when I was a child? Perhaps both. And perhaps this is also why I am drawn to Byron's counsel as well.

Last time after visiting Hazel I told my son, Paul, that I had broken my solitude. He sensed that I had not quite overcome my guilt, even though my visit had been especially satisfying. He did not know I had promised myself this venture would be as pure a solitude as I could ensure. In the wisdom of youth he assured me that what happens is what was supposed to happen. Then he astutely reminded me that Thoreau had three chairs in his cabin in anticipation of company. Paul not only allowed me to forgive myself, but also uplifted me with his eighteen year old insight. I felt proud that he was my son.

This afternoon I decided to take advantage of the calm and go walking. In my jacket pockets were a tin cup and a spoon. My only pie plate was glass. At the last moment I succumbed to Hazel's advice. What *if* I met a bear?

The sky and lake were the same muted grays I knew last February. The world seemed like a giant painting where the artist had swathed soft gray strokes across the top and bottom of the canvas. The calm horizontal strokes spoke to my mood and the quiet surrounding me. I felt particularly serene and free of the "shoulds" and "musts" which too easily accompany me. I had no guilt that I should be writing, or attending to the clutter in the cabin, or checking for frozen pipes. Somehow I permitted these labors to wait.

When I turned into the woods, tiny snowflakes began falling. Undaunted, I followed the leaf strewn paths. After awhile I stopped to survey the landscape. The palette of gray, russet, ebony, and white was exquisite. Reveling in the beauty, I took a deep breath. A pungent smell of decaying leaves filled my nostrils. Invigorated by my senses, I resumed walking. I felt weightless and free. My spirits soared. Not until I leaned over to evade a tree branch did I remember the tin cup and spoon when they nudged my ribs. Without a care I dismissed bears from my mind. Never had one been spotted on the island.

The wispy snowflakes wet my face and speckled my jacket. They were just beginning to whiten the earth. As I approached an open area of the woods I was amazed to see what appeared to be Queen Anne's lace in the distance. Knowing this was absurd, I moved closer. Countless young saplings had cobwebs laced in their delicate branch tops. Each had captured snowflakes to create a doily like pattern. At a distance the illusion of flowers was remarkable. The woods took on an aspect of gaiety and merrymaking. It was a landscape I had never seen. Enchanted, I lingered in its freshness. It was a monoprint. An original. I wished I had brought my camera, but now I realize a copy would diminish what I saw. I suspected its life span was probably measured in hours. Then without warning my attention moved to my cold feet and the darkening sky. I headed home quickly, now and then stopping to gather kindling.

Today was one of those I yearned to inscribe into stone, into something substantive. Something that could not be changed or lost. And so I sit here writing in an attempt to preserve my impressions. Outside the snow is taking the shape of each leaf   something like when strawberries are rolled in powdered sugar. You still know there are strawberries under the whiteness.

Now as I recount the day's simple pleasures of flowing spigots, Hazel's warmth and humor, and the exquisite woodland walk, I almost sense I should do penance for being given such pleasure. Here I am living as I please and offering nothing in return. Why do we sometimes feel guilty when life is especially sweet or tender? Could it be our need to share? Occasionally on these pilgrimages into solitude, I have questioned if it was right to leave my family. Should I have expected them to take on my responsibilities while I enjoyed their absence in pursuit of my goals? There is no question I acted responsibly. I left no one stranded or in need of me. Perhaps I am not discerning the difference between indulgent pleasures and personal satisfaction.

We occasionally drift through a day half in a trance, half in lethargy. Such a day was this. I slept fitfully last night and suspect the culprit was the coffee I consumed. I awakened tired. I prodded myself to make breakfast and shower. Disgusted with my lethargy, I went outside hoping to dispel it. Somehow I shoulder the belief that "to rest is to rust." This was once ascribed to me, and I have never forgotten it. I seldom allow myself the privilege of being tired and doing nothing. Yet there have been times here when I did, and I cannot deny I found them nurturing. However, this morning I was so tired I returned within minutes. I was unable to muster any energy and fell asleep on the red and tan checkered couch.

Scratching noises in the kitchen awakened me. I got up to investigate and discovered I have a cabin mate. He just scurried again past my feet, headed to feast on the d Con I had set by the refrigerator. The mouse is just a baby. His small gray face has dark eyes as glossy as polished onyx, and a sienna streak runs down his back. His audacious behavior reflects his immaturity. Experienced mice run along walls. Not across rooms.

The silence today has been unbroken except for the hum of the refrigerator and the mouse's soft skittering. And now and then, the pump has come on in the well house after I have run water or flushed the toilet. I have seen no one on the lake. Wilson's resort is closed to the northeast. The few private cabins are shut down. Don Abner, who lives behind us, rarely comes to this part of Whitefish Lake. A nurse caring for her invalid mother lives in the old Hansen place near our landing on the mainland. I only see her in summer when she mows. And Hazel stays cocooned in her little white house across the lake.

I have a new appreciation for the silence I have found here. Recently I read about George Hempton who has been recording what little silence is left in the world. This island however, does not meet his standards for "quiet places." We are less than eight miles from a road, less than two miles from power lines, and less than fifty miles from an airport. I am fully aware summers and springs here do not qualify for his "quiet places" with the abundance of manmade sounds streaking across the lake and cutting down trees and blades of grass. But in autumn and winter this island approaches what Hempton calls the experience of "pure listening." I have known moments when there was only silence.

Tonight the sky was clear for the first time since I arrived. Pegasus was visible, and a waning moon rose to stroke the lake in a band of white brushmarks, reminiscent of Monet's red strokes in "Impression: Sunrise." Planets, stars, and galaxies gazed down at me from their great distances.

Since childhood the lesson the universe has repeatedly taught me has been the obvious one many of us have experienced that of man's insignificance. I remembered there was a psalm pertaining to this and found it in our Bible. In Psalm 8.3 4, King David wrote, "When I consider Thy heavens, the work of Thy fingers, the moon and the stars which Thou hast ordained; what is man that Thou art mindful of him?" Yes, we are humbled each time we gaze at the cosmos. We yearn to know the creator of such a universe and how the laws work which govern it. Our human limitations clearly point to a creator far greater and wiser than we.

I mused that for centuries mankind has attempted to explain his universe and the meaning of life. Creation myths and deities arose in most ancient societies. With the advent of Christianity, "Almighty God" reigned as creator, and instilled life with meaning and purpose through his Son. Even today, humankind continues to search for the source of creation and an understanding of God.

I believe the source of creation was God. There is no doubt in my mind of His existence. Yet my ordinary reasoning cannot demonstrate this. Without question my sense of sight informs me this world and cosmos exist. But God is a different matter. I can only claim I see His *hand* in the world and universe about me. My belief that God exists rests on my faith. Because I conceive Him to be all knowing, infinitely loving, and limitless in His power, only He could have created this world and mankind, its complex evolution, its amazing laws.

People have unquestionably been spiritual beings down through the ages. We have sought and still seek an understanding of our relationship to the world and to God. In the secular world we inhabit today, it is difficult to hold onto the wonder and mystery of our spiritual dimension. Many question if it even matters or has any relevance. I believe it does.

The spiritual life speaks to a transformation that is informed by faith. Because we are a people who value denotative thinking, spiritual matters suffer. Essentially faith in God is connotative. It is not precise.

It is not literal or subject to proof. I think there are many people like myself people yearning to keep sight of a God from whom life derives meaning.

I sense my journey is a solitary one. In the silence of contemplating why mankind was created and what our lives ultimately mean, I believe the answers lie in the spiritual realm. There are pitfalls familiar to us all. We become distracted by life's expectations and demands. Thus we become distracted from what we voice as important. I was reminded of this when David called this summer, when his faith was vital and urgent. I have been immersed in the spiritual writings of Thomas Merton, a Trappist monk, as well as those of Bernadette Roberts, a contemplative, and Miester Eckhart, a theologian and Christian mystic from the 14th century. Their spiritual journeys, like my son's, reminded me that the spiritual life is the instrument for mankind to transcend this material world. Only through communion with God can we know the ineffable gift of His grace and love. Only through a turning away from the "self" can we begin to know the sublime transformation God offers.

Tonight I feel as if I have been aroused from sleep. My eyes are trying to accommodate to the spiritual light I have been shutting out. I cannot expect to reach the pinnacle of spiritual transformation without making the climb with my eyes open.

Each time I have come to this island, I have felt its unique character was pregnant with possibilities if I experienced it alone. I have been a seeker of paradise of inner peace and of harmony with the world. But have I in fact been seeking God? There is no question that my solitude on this island has provided insight, or that I have experienced moments of a profound oneness with the natural world. I believe I glimpsed paradise in the emptiness and silence of winter, in the sweet rhythms of spring, and the abundance of summer. But these moments of paradise were fleeting and my life went on as before. Nothing endured. I had been searching for paradise in the quiet of solitude on this island. I thought the synthesis of solitude and place would reveal it. Now I realize paradise is more than a sweet harmony with the world and a peaceful state of mind. Paradise is not found in the exterior world, no matter how lovely it seems. It is interior. It seems that the missing link is spiritual. Paradise must be a spiritual awakening which possesses the power to redirect one's life.

THURSDAY OCTOBER 15

I am bone dry. An empty vessel. For over an hour I have been sitting here on the living room floor gazing out the window, waiting for the moon so I could write. I watched it rise last night and I find its symbolism engages me. In some inexplicable way I believed its presence would fill and inspire me. Does it not possess an aspect of fertility, and speak to women as it unifies them with water in their eternal cycles? But it never appeared. Does this absence of lunar light reflect my emptiness tonight? All day my impressions and thoughts have been disconcerting and confusing. Just a few minutes ago I urged myself to walk over to Poplar Cabin to check for ice in the water. In the darkness I heard a moan. I peered into the black night but saw nothing; nor did I hear the sound again. Now I wonder if I imagined it or uttered it myself. As I was leaving on this errand, I glanced toward the lake. Two lights were aimed toward the island. Who would be on the lake in 27°F weather? By the time I returned to Homestead Cabin the lights had disappeared. Did I imagine them as well?

This afternoon I hiked in the woods. I left the path and happened upon great "bones" in an opening. In reality, they were merely fallen birches, but their amazing configurations suggested ribcages, spinal columns, tibias, and fibulas. Their graveyard was encircled by living trees gazing at their own future lying at their feet. The sight so unnerved me I took off running in search of the path. I thought I heard a gunshot. Turning toward its sound, a second crack filled the woods. I watched my first tree fall on its own accord.

I went to Blackduck early this morning for Amoxicillin. Tony kindly called in the prescription. I have unfortunately developed a urinary tract infection. I suppose this explains why I felt so tired and lethargic yesterday. The pharmacist called me by name before he could know who I was. I was waiting by the counter when he said, "You must be Judy Smithson. Your prescription is ready." I did not stay long enough to ask how he knew me. Driving home I pulled off the road to photograph a tamarack pine I noticed on my way over. As I crawled under a barbed wire fence to gain a better perspective, my mind unexpectedly turned to the baby mouse who kept me company last night. I was filled with remorse for killing him while he believed he had found "paradise" in the aqua blue d Con. Then I began musing if that little mouse, the pharmacist, the tamarack, and I were one with God. I remembered Meister Eckhart's observation that "Being is God's circle and in this circle all creatures exist. Everything that is in God is God."

As I try to make sense of these experiences, I have the feeling I am looking into a lenticular screen where the messages are doubly convex. I cannot trust my perceptions. Perhaps I read Merton, Roberts, and Eckhart in too close a succession. There is no question their mystical experiences and revelations have been consuming me. Or perhaps, I am being given a glimpse of my son's tormented world where he asks, "Mom, how do you know what is real? How do I understand why my mind feels like a door which cannot close and shut out all the voices? Why do I feel like someone is planting seeds in my brain?" His earlier spiritual euphoria and confidence are beginning to fragment. I had worried they might. With uncertainties and misperceptions again invading his consciousness, I am afraid. For him and for me. I was beginning to dare to hope David *could* recover. I had convinced myself I had accepted the loss of the David I once knew and that a "better" David might emerge. Suddenly today, I was forced to confront that not only are my hopes for him terribly fragile, but also my well being is no more certain than his. Is it possible I too am vulnerable to losing my grasp of reality? Who am I? What other faces lie in secret under that which I know?

It always astounds me how feeling good enables one to recover a positive outlook. I awakened refreshed. The morning chores of bringing in logs, opening spigots, and flushing toilets were completed quickly. Breakfast dishes were neatly stacked in the dish rack. The floor swept, clothes folded. Order reigned in the cabin. Outside a brisk wind re arranged the leaf cover, mimicking my vigor.

Like others before, today challenged me with an unexpected hurdle. Late this afternoon I broke the shear pin on the Yamaha motor when I set out to visit Hazel. The powerful wind blew me back into the rocky shore. I could go neither forward nor backward. I was marooned. Canoeing was impossible. I phoned Byron, but there was no answer. The only other person I knew to call was Don Abner who lives on the bay behind us. It was Don who boated us over here ten years ago. His son, Jamie, answered. I asked for Don but learned he would not be back until 8 p.m. I was dismayed until I realized the voice on the phone was not a child's. The last time I saw Jamie he was six. Quick arithmetic informed me he would be sixteen now. I described my dilemma. Jamie offered to come right over said he "knew" about motors. He arrived in minutes, removed the motor and took off the propeller. I had guessed correctly. The shear pin was broken in half, but a new 'one was needed. Then I remembered Tony always kept an extra one on the motor. Jamie found it inside the cover and in minutes I was no longer a prisoner. I ran up to the cabin and found I had ten dollars in my purse. I handed the bill to Jamie. He had willingly come over in 28°F wind to help a woman he did not remember. A surprised grin lit up his face. There could not have been two happier souls on the lake.

After my accident, I had phoned Hazel. She had been watching me through her telescope and witnessed my predicament. Now I called her again to tell her I could come. When she opened her door an appetizing aroma of onions also welcomed me. Convinced I would need nourishment after my cold ordeal, Hazel had made me dinner – beef stir fry, rice, and a pot of vegetables. Overcome by her generosity and kindness, I impulsively hugged her. I think it surprised her, but within a second she embraced me back with the affection of a beloved friend. It was one of the warmest hugs of my life. We stepped back and smiled at one another. Hazel looked splendid. She was wearing her favorite denim jumper and a royal blue turtleneck. Her intelligent blue eyes were sparkling with pleasure under her cropped white hair. For the first time I noticed she had put on lipstick and it was most becoming.

Books, magazines, papers, and mail bedecked her living room. No decorator could have created a space that better reflected the person who lived in it. The cornucopia was the Hazel I knew a substantial woman, both physically and intellectually, engaged with the abundance of life.

She would not allow me to clear the dining room table concealed by her papers. "I might lose them forever if I don't do it," she laughed. Dinner was delicious, though she fretted the meat could be tenderer. I reassured her it was fine. With her company it was a feast. We talked easily and laughed often. We discovered we were both Clinton supporters and she filled me in on the debates I had missed. Our conversation turned to my writing and the books I had been reading. I told her about the spiritual writings which have been engaging me. In particular I mentioned Bernadette Peters' spiritual journey, where she experienced a change of consciousness so profound, she had no awareness of her "self." Her mind became fixed on God. I told Hazel an 85 year old friend of Roberts was surprised to hear of this journey. She had experienced a similar one, believing this change of consciousness was preserved for the final years "was a preparation for a new existence." Hazel had not experienced what I described, but did relate an amazing experience which occurred fifteen years before. Shortly before her husband died of injuries got in a car accident, Hazel was alone in the hospital waiting room where she recalled communicating spiritually with "Chum," that his injuries from their car accident had left him severely handicapped. Hazel assured him she had figured out how they would manage, and if he wished to "go" she would be all right. At that moment she saw her husband's spirit enter the room, pause, and depart. Hazel knew he had "heard" her and made his decision. She glanced at her watch and learned later he had died at the precise moment she saw his spirit.

I am convinced that the human mind is the most challenging frontier we have left to explore and not just in its immense possibilities, but also in its dysfunctions which I know to be poorly understood.

I departed tonight physically and emotionally nourished, intellectually stimulated. What a marvelous tonic Hazel is. I will miss her.

My day is now over. And likewise these pilgrimages. A light snow is falling which seems to be a particularly fitting finale. This log cabin will soon listen to winter's silences and know its harsh cold. The landscape will become a blank canvas recording the tales of the creatures who remain their struggles and triumphs. My tracks will be missing for a time... but I shall return, alone, to keep sight of who I am.

I came here to experience solitude in the natural world my notion of paradise. I discovered solitude is a catalyst, not an end in itself. It provides a habitat for self discovery, but solitude's essence resides *within* us, wherever we might be.

As I look back at my pilgrimages to this island, I realize what a profound adventure I have lived. I traveled into remarkable realms stretching from abysses of despair to peaks of joy. I wonder if one of my quests into solitude was about my capacity to overcome adversity and discover who I am.

Now I know I am a capable human being who has the capacity to handle life's adversities. I also discovered that the offerings I was given in the natural world became significant events. Now I must make the best of what I have learned. Our daring begins from within.

The future demands that I engage in caring for what I value and for whom I value. My life ahead holds promise.

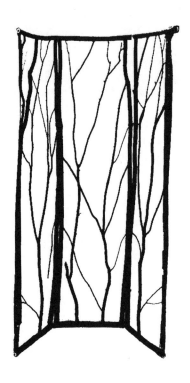

Pan's Screen

Notes on Willow Pieces

"Woodstove" is a structure of willow, plywood and stovepipe — similar to the stove in the cabin. Not only was the stove's warmth vital to my survival, it also offered me companionship. Its palpable form intimates an importance to me beyond its function.

"Exterior Landscape" speaks to the discovery that in the natural world my thoughts were outside myself, free and joyful. The willow branches are as unencumbered as I felt

"Interior Landscape" reveals the discovery that inside the walls of the cabin my thoughts were also interior — confined by memory. The branchless willow boughs bound by a leather thong reflect the sense of containment.

"Emergence" suggests the fruits given when two kinds of thinking merge. The dogwood branches cradle a nest and the egg within it. This piece evokes the birth of insight and knowledge.

"Pan's Screen" pays homage to Pan, god of nature in Greek mythology. One summer afternoon a bird's song led me to imagine Pan playing his pipes. This screen, fashioned from delicate willow branches, reveals the beauty and fragility of the natural world.

Judy Smithson, November, 1995

It is the last weekend of October. Four years have passed since I recorded my final journal entry in October 1992. Once again I am at the island, but this time encircled by family. We have come to close the cabin for winter. The old pattern of women's work and men's work has reasserted itself. Tony, David, and Paul have pulled in the dock, sailboat, and pontoon. Tomorrow they will dismantle the plumbing. My primary tasks are the housekeeping chores here in Homestead Cabin – scrubbing the bathroom and kitchen, emptying the refrigerator, clearing the cabinets of perishables, vacuuming the rugs, stripping the beds – a ritual unchanged in our fourteen years of closing the island. I do not begrudge theses simple chores. They are good in themselves and soothe one's spirits in their undertaking. Moreover, they bring closure to the island and another season.

This afternoon the chainsaw's whine pierced the silence as Tony felled a dead elm in the woods. The boys and I labored together stacking the logs in the porch. I found comfort in observing the logs rise up to the level of the screen. They promise warmth when I return alone this winter.

The island landscape smells of autumn. Woodsmoke in the air. Pungent earth under my feet. Damp mottled leaves in ochers and umbers mask the forest floor. Today they clung to my boots as I walked the familiar paths. The spare trees framing me rose up like Giacommetti's tall thin figures. They possessed a fleeting presence standing among their former attire. Intermittently I spotted tufts of grasses pushing through the leaf cover and mosses blanketing fallen trees, offering unexpected glimpses of green. The vibrant color seemed incongruous in this monochromatic landscape. As I approached Birchwood Cabin, I kneeled to examine a stand of Indian pipes, now black and erect. Last August I joyfully discovered them under the shade of a fir. Their former translucent summer whites seem a distant memory now. I arose slowly, inhaling an earthy dank aroma.

It is good to be back in this place of silence. No birdsong, no loquacious squirrels, no rustling of leaves reached my ears. No loons called from the lake. They have departed for the warm waters of the Chesapeake Bay and the Carolinas. Like this island, the loons will be mute until the return of spring.

As I write tonight, I find myself gazing across the lake. Hazel's house waits in darkness. It cannot know she will not be returning. For two decades, Hazel arrived here when the ice went out in May and departed for her daughter's home in New York when the first snow whitened the landscape. Fragile health has closed this chapter of her life. Her lake solitude will now exist only in her memory.

Early today I boated across the lake to visit her home once more, drawn by the rich memories residing there. Her white shingled house was locked tight, curtains drawn except in the study and kitchen. Peering in the windows, I could see a few remnants of her years here. Dusty shelves of books and periodicals and a bulging shopping bag of papers transported me back to our rich conversations in summers gone by. We had been two women of different generations experiencing the fruits of solitude, on parallel shores.

The yard alone seemed unchanged. Hazel's giant thermometer still hung on the tree outside her kitchen window, registering 36 degrees Fahrenheit. Beside the forlorn flowerbeds, three faded plastic sunflowers stood immobile, waiting for a breeze to set them spinning. The weathered birdfeeder was deserted. Any birdseed it once offered was long consumed. Silence permeated the deserted landscape, and possessed a hollowness, a restlessness I did not perceive on our island. For an instant I felt a sense of expectancy, as if Hazel were approaching the door to greet me. Foolish, wishful imaginings.

I particularly miss seeing Hazel's lights at night. They would tell me she was reading or perhaps sipping a cup of the green tea she believed controlled her blood pressure better than any medicine. It occurs to me that I am being confronted by one of the few certainties in our lives. Nothing stays the same.

It is morning now. Blue traces of sky are visible as a northwest wind scatters yesterday's cloud cover. The rarefied air energizes me and lifts my spirits. A new day awaits. There is no place for mourning. My friendship with Hazel will endure. I will endure. As I work here in the kitchen, a shaft of sunlight dances across my paper. Is this not enough for the moment?

As I look back through my journal entries, I am astonished how many other changes have come, both in my external life and within myself. I am now writing in a time of reflection which offers the perspective of distance. Beside me rests the first printing of this book, a palpable object which arose from my sojourns into solitude. The book signifies a change in my external life. Writing this epilogue, I clearly recall my musings one summer night four years ago:

"I yearn to find if I can write or visually create work I value enough to publish or send to juried exhibitions."

And, a few paragraphs later:

"I can hear the evening chorus outside the cabin. Each creature is singing its song. Each creature knows its work. How good it would be to possess such certain knowledge."

Today I marvel at how resolutions to these concerns gradually emerged. The solitude I encountered here not only elicited insights and healing, but also led to unexpected opportunities – to a new definition of who I am and what I do. Somehow I emerged as a writer.

Shortly after I completed my four visits to the island, I was invited to speak to the Alice Mayo Society, a group of women whose husbands are Mayo Clinic staff members. Some of the women knew of my journeys into solitude and believed my experiences would be of interest. I accepted their invitation.

I decided to read from my journal rather than attempt to recapitulate my experiences. It seemed that the authentic account of the experiences lay in the journal entries themselves – recorded as I lived them. I further decided to accompany my reading with slides, which I would make from the photographs I had taken over the course of my visits. The necessity to narrow my focus led to choosing one season for this talk. I selected "Winter," the season when I embarked on my first journey and discovered the importance of solitude.

As I walked to the podium that afternoon, I remember my heart racing out of control. My mouth was dry, my throat tight. Rarely had I spoken before groups. I was grateful when the room was darkened. I could see no faces. The darkness offered me a welcome anonymity. Soon a calmness ensued. I could swallow and begin. Speaking the familiar words soothed me and drew my attention from myself. I would survive this. In those forty minutes the silence in the room was unbroken except by my voice. After I finished the lights were again turned on, but the silence continued. Dismay enveloped me. I chided myself for accepting the invitation. How could I have put myself in such a vulnerable position? I suppose I had been flattered at being asked to speak, and believed my experiences would be interesting to women like myself.

I thanked the audience for their attention and offered to answer questions. Within seconds applause filled my ears. My relief was immeasurable. Perhaps what I had confronted was of value. Hands shot up. The first question asked was, "Where can I find your book?" "There is no book, only this journal," I answered.

The women's responses that afternoon initiated a new direction in my life. I discovered my confrontations with myself, my marriage and children, my uncertain future, were all shared experiences. Most surprising were the positive remarks about my writing. My venture into solitude, I gratefully realized, had offered me the setting, the time and the means, to arrive at this very moment.

Afterwards, two older women approached me. They eagerly shared their stories of solitude. In some inexplicable way, my journal elicited memories long passed in their lives. When I was alone, a younger professional woman walked up to me. She told me she had been seeking help in coping with the difficulties and uncertainties in her life. She remarked, "Your talk has convinced me to take some time alone for myself. I've thought about this for awhile now, but got discouraged when friends didn't think it was a good idea. Now I'm certain it is." These women and others provided me with the inspiration and confidence to seek publication.

Knowing nothing about getting published, I began researching how to approach such a task. I discovered it begins with a query letter, describing your manuscript. I further learned an entire manuscript is sent only by invitation.

I purchased a reference book listing publishers around the country, including descriptions of the kind of books each printed. After discovering the major presses worked primarily through agents, I chose to send my letters to small presses receptive to new writers. My greatest difficulty was finding a fit. My journal format and reflective writing did not precisely correspond with any of the publishers' descriptions. Finally I mailed out seven query letters to the presses whose focus most closely reflected my work.

I received seven rejections. I rewrote my query letter, chose eight more presses, and enclosed five pages from my winter writings. I received five rejection letters and thee manuscript requests. This hopeful period ended in rejection letters as well. One publisher commented my writing was not "feminist" enough. Another said, "I think readers will have trouble relating to your experience. Most people do not have an island." However, I was encouraged by other publishers to keep trying. One kind editor wrote, "You have written a beautiful book... The problem, as I see it, is that the prose leans too much to the literary and the insights too much to the personal.... This is a book worthy of publication." But I felt beaten. This editor did not know my list of possible publishers was exhausted. I thought of my writer friend who also received rejection letters. She saved them with a sense of humor and pride. Remembering her response heartened me.

Throughout this time, friends and family continued to encourage me and prevented my slipping into total despair. Further invitations arose to read from my work. It occurred to me how vital affirmation is in our lives. It preserves our dignity, nourishes our souls. The potential for profound good awaits in each of us, merely through a few words to another human being.

In my kitchen one afternoon, I was sorting papers stored in a wicker basket on the counter. I found a clipping I had cut out of the Star Tribune. It was a review of Eugene McCarthy's volume of poetry *And Time Began*. In his closing remarks, the reviewer thanked Lone Oak Press in Rochester for publishing this kind of work. I had been given one final possibility. Two weeks passed before I mustered the courage to call. I simply asked the editor at Lone Oak if he would read a few pages from my journal. I hand delivered "Winter" to his door. The following morning, I departed for North Carolina to embark on a journey with my twin sister.

On my return, a letter awaited me from Lone Oak Press. It was an invitation from the editor to meet him for lunch. We met. In his unassuming manner, he said, "If the remainder of the book is equal to 'Winter' I want to publish it." Oh! What joy! "Why?" I whispered. "It made me feel," he answered.

That summer afternoon was the culmination of a two-year journey arising from solitude, but not about solitude. It was about possibilities and affirmation. I had discovered that ordinary people like me, or the women who shared their memories at my first reading, have life experiences that are important. They can be heard, if they are offered.

It is now mid-November and I am back in Rochester. Autumn is running out as it advances into winter with unyielding, purposeful steps. A cold wind moans outside; rain and snow are freezing rapidly. Unexpectedly, I almost slipped on the deck carrying logs in from the garage. It is good to be sitting here in the family room, sheltered from the wrath outside my window and warmed by the fire I laid. The cats also have wisely chosen to stay inside. Electra has taken refuge in the loft, Smokey under the woodstove. Patterns of rippled ice now distort the view from the window. I can scarcely make out some chickadees and two pairs of cardinals consuming the sunflower seeds I set out this morning. I sit in wonder at how they endure this relentless weather.

As I write in this season of reflection, I ponder the interior changes solitude makes possible in our lives. Clearly it offers a haven from the demands of the external world, providing a place where the psyche can re-center and heal.

Solitude offered me an immersion into calm. It provided time for introspection. Time for silence. Time to walk. Time to confront my life. Time to heal. But being healed or becoming whole is more than a kind of recovery from the world's demands and expectations. It is the deep satisfaction of knowing and accepting who we are. It is an awareness of what is significant in life.

This past summer I received a letter from a physician who had recently read my book. He wrote, "So reflective, peaceful and descriptive, that I sighed several times for the opportunity to escape the daily grind, phone calls, and To Do lists... Your experiences convinced me to return to the North Carolina Outer Banks alone... to revisit the small towns my father and I frequented years ago.."

A yearning for solitude has probably been experienced by most of us. The necessity for it is becoming clearer as we observe the alarming increase of stress that compromises the lives around us.

Solitude clearly changed my life. It was in my spring solitude that I discovered the necessity of relinquishing my dependency on others. This insight led me to move forward more secure in my ability to survive, to cope, to contribute. I began growing up. My book was described by one reader as a "coming of age" book. Perhaps it is. Unquestionably, solitude was the catalyst which spurred my growth. Anne Morrow Lindbergh also understood this when she wrote, "Woman must come of age by herself. She must find her true center alone." This is not a new idea, but one which needs to be shared with each generation. The solitary journey to wholeness includes all of us – men and women alike.

So how am I different now? How did my immersion into solitude change the manner in which I live? Simply put, I was given a new awareness. In my last journal entry in "Winter" I wrote, "If paradise is a heightened capacity to live, I am sitting in heaven." I wondered then how I would hold onto this "heightened living" when I returned to the familiar strain of sustaining the demands in my life. I discovered there is no mystery. "Heightened living" merely requires a conscious awareness of what is significant, what is graceful.

Solitude was a wise teacher, revealing its necessity in my life. Coming home, I clearly recognized my need for time to focus, to create. Now I take it, saying "no" to lesser priorities with conviction and no apologies.

I further understood the importance I placed on a warm relationship with my children, too often jeopardized by unsolicited advice. When our children reach adulthood, parenting must change. I am now striving to listen more. To encourage. Such a simple mistake as comparing myself or my children with others was exposed. Distress and disappointment always ensue. I am more gentle with myself. And with them.

The importance of responding to others' difficulties or achievements was illuminated as well. A letter or phone call of concern or congratulations is so easy to dismiss as insignificant. Yet each can generate surprising warmth. Just this minute, I received a phone call from the mother of a close friend of my daughter Molly. She called to thank me for "sharing" Molly with their family this Thanksgiving. I sit here enriched by her thoughtful awareness that we would miss Molly.

These examples of changed behavior in my life may seem trite, commonplace. But are they? On my kitchen wall is *Desiderata,* a treatise of wisdom found in Old Saint Paul's Church in Baltimore, dated 1692. It says, "Go placidly among the noise and haste, and remember what peace there may be in silence. As far as possible without surrender, be on good terms with all persons..." My journeys revealed the necessity both for solitude and for caring relationships.

Awareness of what is significant in life has not only affected my relationships but also the ordinary tasks I confront each day. Now I can find pleasure in the trivial. I enjoy the ritual of folding laundry fresh and warm from the dyer. The satisfaction in smoothing the rumpled sheets on my bed. The simple labor of carrying logs inside that my family cut. The calming motion of sweeping the porch. Former pedestrian tasks have become healing.

The solitary walks I took each season revealed yet another awareness. My senses were keener and I was awakened to notice beauty in the infinite patterns of bark textures or the soft rhythmic hooting of the barred owl from deep in the woods. Simple observations, but ones I had missed in the company of others.

Each season revealed something significant in the ordinary. Winter's silent perfection created a "cathedral." Spring's "fragrant grasses and flowers, darting butterflies and bees," placed me in the Elysian Fields. In summer's riot of green, the sweet song of a bird led me to hear Pan playing his pipes. Autumn's earthy aromas laced the bracing air, and I inhaled perfume for the gods. Ordinary moments became extraordinary and significant – a synthesis of my senses and my imagination. Was it possible to discover such moments in Rochester where my life was inundated with "To Do" lists?

Yes. The simple requirement is to take time to enter the natural world. To get out of our cars, our houses, our workplaces, the malls. Nature's gifts are freely given. Her significant moments are ours if we let go of the clutter stifling our imaginations. Pegasus awaits our gaze in the night sky. The mythology surrounding him has inspired poets since antiquity. His mystery can transform the night into a place of sublimity, if we dare to imagine.

On a table in my living room rest a deer skull and antlers washed clean by rains and snows, bleached by the sun. They are palpable gifts from nature, given to me while hiking on a friend's farm. Other skeletal bones – tibias, femurs, scapulas – were strewn near the skull. Tiny teeth marks show me the deer's death ensured ongoing life to the field mice and other creatures. The long decayed carcass had nourished the earth on which I stood. The cycle of death begetting life raised my consciousness, made me consider the wonder of ongoing creation. Each time I enter my living room, this significant moment returns and I am reminded of the awe I experienced that afternoon.

Other gifts are not palpable, but fleeting moments we can only hold in our memories. I received such a gift this autumn. I was walking at sunset along Mayowood Road here in Rochester. The evening sky was a curtain of deep cobalt blue. As the sun slipped behind the hills, I glanced at an oak to my left. The tree was blazing scarlet. Its great outstretched arms glowing like embers. There was something familiar in this sublime image. It was later I remembered Piet Mondrian's painting, *Red Tree*. I wondered if he had once encountered this same exquisite moment or imagined it ...

Clearly this world we inhabit excels at "sensory overload." So much to absorb or discard. So much to consider or dismiss. So much to do or undo. We can come to feel we are falling into an abyss of chaos. How do we cope in a culture bombarding us with its incessant noise and demands?

In the course of my walks this autumn, I encountered numerous furry woolly bears. It occurred to me that my immersion into the quiet of solitude was something like this caterpillar stage of these soon-to-be Isabella tiger moths. Life at the island, alone, was calm, focused, slow moving. But in time I knew I would emerge to fly back into this world racing to – where? Somehow I needed to hold on to some of that calm where I reclaimed my "self." Where the wonders of nature soothed me.

In other times, when life is fractious and I stagger with vertigo, my solitude seems like a dream, the island a mythical place. In such moments I recognize it is time to return to solitude. If the island is not an option, a walk alone is. Just an hour can be healing. Entering the natural world I can honor the whisper of a hummingbird – and life is sweet again.

On the first day of my winter sojourn, I mused that paradise might be discovered in the synthesis of nature and solitude. As a counterpoint, I referred to Jack Kerouac's characters Dean and Sal, who sought paradise in "excitement, movement, and stimulants." In another of Kerouac's books, I met Ray and Japhy, who discovered a world the antithesis of Dean's and Sal's. On Ray's arrival at Desolation Peak to spend a summer alone he observed:

> "Lo, in the morning I woke up and it was beautiful blue sunshine sky and I went out in my alpine yard and there it was, everything Japhy said it was. Hundreds of miles of pure snow-covered rocks and virgin lakes and high timber...
>
> "Suddenly I realized I was truly alone... and nobody could criticize. The little flowers grew everywhere around the rocks, and no one had asked them to grow or me to grow.
>
> "... It seemed a golden festival of rejoicement was taking place. In my diary I wrote, 'Oh, I'm happy!' In the late day peaks I saw hope. Japhy had been right."

In spite of the cacophony we hear, in spite of the stresses we endure, we can discover insights and healing, in solitude. It is my hope that you will find your own version of my remote northern island and experience the fruits of solitude.

Photograph of Judy Smithson on back cover by
Tony Smithson